CALIFORNIA'S
Historic Haunts

A Planet Paranormal Guide
to the Other Side

BRIAN CLUNE WITH BOB DAVIS

4880 Lower Valley Road • Atglen, PA 19310

Other Schiffer Books on Related Subjects:
Philadelphia's Haunted Historic Walking Tour, 978-0-7643-4437-4, $16.99
Haunted Historic Greensboro, 978-0-7643-3174-9, $16.99
Virginia's Haunted Historic Triangle: Williamsburg, Yorktown, Jamestown, & Other Haunted Locations, 978-0-7643-3746-8, $19.99
America's Historic Haunts, 978-0-7643-3700-0, $29.99

Designed by Brenda McCallum
Cover design by John Cheek
Type set in Yukon Gold/!Sketchy Times/Times New Roman
ISBN: 978-0-7643-4706-1
Printed in the United States of America

Published by Schiffer Publishing, Ltd.
4880 Lower Valley Road
Atglen, PA 19310
Phone: (610) 593-1777; Fax: (610) 593-2002
E-mail: Info@schifferbooks.com

For our complete selection of fine books on this and related subjects, please visit our website at www.schifferbooks.com. You may also write for a free catalog.

This book may be purchased from the publisher. Please try your bookstore first.

We are always looking for people to write books on new and related subjects. If you have an idea for a book, please contact us at proposals@schifferbooks.com.

Schiffer Publishing's titles are available at special discounts for bulk purchases for sales promotions or premiums. Special editions, including personalized covers, corporate imprints, and excerpts can be created in large quantities for special needs. For more information, contact the publisher.

DEDICATION

To my wife, Terri, who had to put up with me being
gone countless hours investigating the locations in this
book, and then having to endure endless jabber while
the book was being written, rewritten, and rewritten
again. If that was not bad enough, I then forced her to
not only be my final spell-checker, but to help with
the final edit. I could not have done this without you,
baby! Yes Dear: **Brian Clune**

To my mother and father, Betty and Bill, for their years
of patience, understanding, and support. I only wish
they could have lived to enjoy our book. To my wife,
Miyu, and son, Nicky, for tolerating my unusual
pursuits and encouraging me to continue with those
pursuits nonetheless. To my daughter, Katrina, I would
not be here if it wasn't for you. Thanks for being my
first ghost-hunting buddy. I love you guys with all my
heart: **Bob Davis**

ACKNOWLEDGMENTS

We would like to thank our intrepid friends and
teammates, Caitlyn Quinn and Laurel Blackwell. You
helped make this adventure truly fun and memorable.
We look forward to many more excursions into the
other realm with you by our side.

Contents

Forewords

I met Bob Davis in 2006 while participating in a paranormal expedition of the *Queen Mary*, which is permanently docked in Long Beach, California. I was already involved in researching locations that are reported to be haunted for nearly fifteen years at that point, and Bob's quick wit and knowledge led us to becoming close friends. He soon introduced me to Brian Clune and other Southern California residents with a similar interest, and a loose group of us traveled throughout the state and into neighboring towns just outside of California's borders. We were in search of answers to the same questions that have been asked for the millennia, but specifically we wanted to know: Just what is it that remains in a location when the original inhabitants suddenly leave?

Bob and Brian organized road trips that were more than just casual explorations; they became real missions with a purpose. The process of collecting and analyzing data was something we all were learning along the way, and sleep was merely an option that we usually ignored. In some of the places we visited, it would feel like we hit a paranormal jackpot. Sometimes it is just an eerie presence that you can feel, but on occasion you can record what seems like subtle communication from people that evade your normal senses.

It has been my experience that locations with a tragic past seem to yield more of this type of evidence, but there are no set rules to follow when investigating a historical location in an effort to establish contact with what some would call communication with discarnate personalities. Perhaps the specific conditions that must be met in order to record visual or audio evidence of what is often referred to as a haunting will someday be discovered. Maybe the process is more dependent on synergistic personalities instead of environmental factors. In any case, Bob and Brian have what it takes to properly document their experiences, carefully record what is considered by many to be evidence of communication with the spirit realm, and complete the tedious research related to the history of the locations they have visited. They present their findings in a manner that entertains the reader even while sending a shiver down your spine.

Bob opened his home to some of us in the paranormal community, and in the process he has become a hub for many of us to stay in contact with each other as the decades pass from one to the next. Along the way, he and Brian took the reins of an ambitious project to publicize their own work and the work of others, and Planet Paranormal has become a popular Internet destination for those who want to share and learn about what may be just beyond what we take for granted to be the complete picture. As many in the community have gained experience, we have also acquired more sophisticated technology to further extend our senses beyond what we can see, hear, or even feel — but it always circles back to the manner in which you choose to interact with those you make contact with, even if you are trying to contact an unseen force. This is where Bob and Brian shine. They remain grounded family men with all the responsibilities faced with raising kids, yet they have remained colleagues throughout the years.

With the meticulous amount of research contained in *California's Historic Haunts*, reading their book is a treat without feeling overly dense. Some of the writing evokes images of peeking into a darkened room, and when you suddenly hear that faint whisper coming from that corner where there is no light, you snap to attention. They never resort to adding fluff to their writing — real world experiences provide everything needed to keep the reader turning each page, just to learn what will happen next. The history of the people and the locations they have included are not always for the faint of heart. War, isolation, blundering medical attempts to treat manic patients, it's all there for the curious reader and sets the stage when they reveal the residual energies that have resulted from the suffering society has imposed on itself while attempting to keep a grip on its population. Their book also treats the reader to some beautiful interaction that they have kept good records of. I have witnessed some of these moments with Bob and Brian; somehow a beacon that attracts a positive force (for lack of a better description) attracts welcome communication. The guys of Planet Paranormal have earned their place in the paranormal community through hard work and careful documentation, so that those who follow their path will know where to look. For the budding paranormal investigator, you have found the book that will lead you in the right direction. For the seasoned researcher, you may find that the incredible attention to detail in *California's Historic Haunts* will shed new light on the people and places that you thought you knew. ~ Bill Murphy

Bill Murphy has been a paranormal investigator since 1992 and has contributed to over 100 radio and television broadcast and magazine articles. His work has been seen on the Biography Channel, the Discovery Channel, and as a key team member of the hit series Fact or Faked: Paranormal Files on the SyFy Network. Throughout his career, Bill has worked with various engineers and experimenters in an effort to explore what difficult to detect information can be obtained by examining the electromagnetic spectrum with custom-made electronics. He is the Science Correspondent for the Lucid Dreaming Exchange, a quarterly magazine devoted to the psychology and experiences of lucid dreamers. Bill's website is www.ghosttown.tv.

Two paranormal pals take you on an amazing journey through time and space as they try to uncover some of histories mysteries. As they investigate haunted destinations that are open to the public throughout California, they inspire and enlighten with their historic approach to haunted places like Alcatraz, Camarillo State Hospital, and the most haunted ship afloat, the *Queen Mary*. These are only a few enticing locations in this amazing and revealing book that we highly recommend.

Brian and Bob use history to help solve discrepancies in perpetuated myths and legends and they use paranormal techniques to fill gaps in the historic records. While on a tour of Alcatraz, through ITC (Instrumental Transcommunication), they were able to substantiate a little-known historic fact about women serving as nurses on the island during a tuberculosis epidemic. As they so aptly point out, history is a powerful tool for unlocking the secrets of the past, especially within the purview of the paranormal. If you want to learn some history, have some ghostly fun, and maybe even frighten yourself by envisioning what awaits you on your next journey to a haunted place, then this book is the perfect resource. You can sit back in the quiet comfort of your living room by a cozy fire, or take your curiosity to another level and plan a road trip to the haunted locations near you; but remember, without this book, your adventure will be a lot harder to plan and execute. Take Bob and Brian for a spin with their book in hand and dare to follow in their footsteps. Oh, and may the spirits always "boo" with you as you visit some of California's most haunted destinations. ~ Rob and Anne Wlodarski, G-Host Publishing (www.ghostpublishingco.com)

Introduction

As many reading this book will notice, we delve into the history of the sites we investigate as deeply as we possibly can. The reason for this is that without the historical knowledge of the location, how can one hope to discover the reasons for a haunting? What are we doing when we research a site for ghosts and the paranormal if not trying to locate one of the historical aspects of the house, business, or piece of land that has peaked our interest?

If you go to one of the sites in this book to get a scare and nothing else and something does occur, we can guarantee that once you get home and are sitting in the safety of your living room, you or one of your friends will inevitably ask the question, "What was that?" What was that indeed? If you have no point of reference, you may never know; however, if you know the background of the location you can postulate a theory based on the history and type of occurrence that took place.

An example could be taken from Alcatraz. While on Alcatraz, Planet Paranormal caught a very clear EVP of a woman in an area where we would have thought no woman would have been. However, when checking into the history of that area of the island, we discovered that at one time a tuberculosis epidemic occurred and a nurse aiding the sick men contracted the disease and was quarantined with the other patients and subsequently died. Without that piece of historical knowledge, we would never have known about this brave woman — or that she was still there trying to communicate with us. Another example is the Banning Museum: It's been reported that Banning had been seen devising military strategy at the house. After reading that chapter in this book, you will see how knowing the history of the home and its owner will dispel that notion.

If you think on it, history is the reason we know where to look for ghosts in the first place. Urban legend, folklore…they have their roots in the location of their origin. How do we know that the ghost of a murdered wife haunts "the last house on the left?" Or that the "Bayou down south" has a voodoo witch casting spells on the unwary? History. If we did not know the history behind Eastern State Prison or Waverly Sanatorium, would we ever think about going to these run-down places just to look at them? No, but the history of their paranormal activity draws us in and holds us captive.

The late psychic Peter James was known for helping the Los Angeles Police Department (LAPD) with murder cases that detectives had given up on. James would go to the crime scene and look for the victims of the murder. If he made contact, he would talk to them about how they were killed. Gathering the history of the crime from those that were there, he would then relate the victim's story to the police. Quite a few crimes were solved in this manner, not just by Mr. James, but by psychics all across the country. History can be and is a powerful tool for unlocking the secrets of the past, especially that of the paranormal.

We also do not delve very deeply into the paranormal activity of the places that we have visited. The reason for this is that we do not want to give too much fuel to the imagination of the investigator. If we were to tell everything that happened during our investigations, then why would one need to go there for themselves? We want the novice investigator to have the thrill of discovering something new on their own. The breath-taking experience of finding that electronic voice phenomenon (EVP) during review or that photo evidence caught on their camera untainted by Planet Paranormal's experience. Hopefully, we have given you just enough to peak your interest without spoiling any surprise that may await you.

As all of the locations in this book are accessible to the general public, it is our hope that you find this guide useful and that you head into the world of spirits with an open mind and kind heart for the souls that await you. One thing to remember: the journey you are about to start is one of your making, so head into it with knowledge and thought and you will find rewards. Go into it with mischief and wrong intent and you may well find that things can turn against you in ways you have never dreamed.

Happy Hunting!

Southern California

The Banning House getting ready for a face-lift.

Banning Residence Museum

For those of us who live in the Los Angeles area, the name Banning is well known; not as the name of the man who is the father of the Port of Los Angeles, but as a small section in the City of Wilmington. Others relate to the name because they had attended Banning High or played their teams; some just know it as a boulevard that will take them to the docks for a day of fishing. Few know that this part of LA was instrumental in the cause of the Civil War or that the man who named Wilmington was a key player in the development of the entire region.

Phineas Banning was born August 19, 1830, in the town of Wilmington, Delaware. Always a restless child, he left home at age thirteen to go to work in the Philadelphia law office of his older brother. Before too long, this office job became tedious and he sought employment on the docks, where he could talk to the sailors coming into port about their adventures in faraway places. So it was no surprise that at the age of twenty-one Banning headed west by ship to Panama, crossed through the jungle to the Pacific Ocean, and made his way to the small town of Los Angeles, California.

It was 1851 when Banning came to the small pueblo on the frontier and set out to make his fortune. Seeing the water around San Pedro, he knew immediately that this was where he wanted to be. He took employment as a clerk at the tiny port pier owned by Spanish Don Sepulveda and his family. At that time, the port was just a small collection of shacks and one wooden wharf — all that was needed for the ships arriving at the time. The Sepulvedas also owned a stage line that served from Los Angeles to the port some twenty miles away.

It didn't take Banning long before he was driving the wagons on the trip between the two small towns. The whole time he was working, he dreamt of seeing fleets of ships at anchor with wagons hauling all the exotic goods from faraway places to market — and it was himself he saw owning those wagons. He would save his money and take on extra work to make his dreams come true and, in short order, he had enough to buy a few wagons and the mules to haul them. At first, he drove the wagons himself — long drives across the desert, cold nights spent in the mountains — until he could hire employees of his own.

In 1853, he took on a partner by the name of Harris Newmark, and this infusion of business allowed Banning to open up a route to Salt Lake, where he traded at the small Mormon outpost. Later, he brokered a deal to be the main supplier for the U.S. Cavalry when they set up Fort Tejon. This required that he build a road for his wagons to traverse and he completed it in plenty of time to serve the troops stationed there.

Banning fell in love with and married the younger sister of one of his first employers, Rebecca Sanford. The couple had eight children; only William, Joseph, and Hancock would survive to adulthood, however. Rebecca would die in childbirth in 1868, along with the infant, which devastated Banning for a time, but, as happens, love found him again when he met Mary Hollister, whose family gave their name to Hollister, California, and he remarried into a wealthy California family. Phineas and Mary had three children, two of whom, Mary and Lucy, would live to adulthood.

Banning was in the process of creating his own town, so he purchased 640 acres of land within site of the harbor and called it "Wilmington" in honor of his birthplace. He approached the federal government and petitioned them to certify the Port of San Pedro as an international harbor. Washington was slow in granting his request, but that didn't stop Phineas Banning. He dredged his own canal to allow heavy freight to be hauled up to his town and within a couple years the first oceangoing vessel anchored in his port. The locals awarded him the honorary title of "Port Admiral," a designation Banning thoroughly enjoyed. It would be another thirteen years before the government, now seeing its potential, would agree to dredge the harbor and fully allow it to become an international port. In 1860, Banning, frustrated over the lack of progress, constructed his own telegraph line to Los Angeles from Wilmington, which finally allowed the port to shed its isolation and truly become part of the world.

Banning was a stout Unionist and abolitionist, but he was also a devout capitalist, so when the Civil War broke out in 1861 he not only saw a way to help the army, but also a way to make a profit as well. Knowing that Fort Tejon was too far away from Los Angeles to be able to respond quickly to the large secessionist population, Banning and his partner, B. D. Wilson, offered to sell a large plot of land to the military for two dollars (one dollar each) — as long as they were awarded the right

The Banning schoolhouse is now used as the visitor's center.

The barn holds many old carriages and is part of the house tour.

The gardens at the Banning house.

We were on vacation in California from New Jersey to visit relatives and had heard about the Banning Museum from a ghost show that we had watched. Being a fan of those types of programs and wanting to have a scare of my own, I took my husband to see this haunted house. When we got there, I was surprised at how urban the surroundings were and wondered if that was going to interfere with us seeing a ghost. We signed up for the tour, but had to wait about 20 minutes for it to start, so we wandered around the gardens and outside the house itself. We finally saw the tour guide come out the back door, so we quickly headed over to get ready to enter the house. We were first taken to the barn, then this little schoolhouse before at last being shown into his mansion. Like I said, after seeing so many shows about this place, I was excited, nervous, and even a little scared entering this place even though there was my husband and four other people with me.

As soon as we entered, I could feel the spirit energy surrounding us. I had the strangest feeling that I was being watched and the hair rose on my arms and the back of my neck. Going upstairs, I could sense that the Banning children were still in their rooms at play and could even tell that the servants were still tending to them. I was beginning to relax a bit when we came back down to the main floor and went into Mr. Banning's office—and there he was standing at his desk with what appeared to be two other men in Civil War uniforms. It looked as if Banning was giving them orders, as the other men seemed to pay close attention to every word the General was saying. I was so shocked by this encounter that the whole rest of the tour is just a blur to me. My husband didn't see a thing, and it seems that no one else on the tour noticed this event, but I am sure that it occurred... as it happened exactly as I had heard from the shows.

~ Beverly Saperstein

Authors Note: As I state in this chapter, Phineas Banning's title of General was strictly ceremonial and held no authority within the ranks of the military. With this in mind, I find it unlikely that this occurrence has any validity and is most likely due to having seen this account on "reality TV," coupled with a highly emotional state from wanting something paranormal to happen. However, it is up to the reader to make that determination.

to supply the new garrison. The government agreed and Fort Drum was built in Wilmington to protect the harbor and the nearby city of Los Angeles. Banning was given an honorary commission as General in the California militia, but this designation held no responsibilities or actual military command; regardless of this, Banning made sure that for the rest of his life, he would be addressed as General Phineas Banning.

When the war ended in 1865, the military kept Drum barracks open for another two years, but it became too expensive to operate and there was very little to protect, so in 1867 they sold back the land to Wilson and Banning for the one dollar they originally paid and auctioned off the buildings. Wilson purchased the hospital and Banning bought some of the other structures and began setting up the area around his home.

It was around this time that Banning set up his small railroad from the port of San Pedro to Los Angeles. Banning had figured on making a fortune running goods from the now busy docks, but it seemed fate would not allow this venture. The Southern Pacific Railroad was expanding and wanted to add a route of its own to the waterfront; this meant the dissolution of the smaller line for that of the other. Banning vehemently protested, but the city, being told by the railroad that they would "turn their streets to grass," relented and Banning lost his route.

Although the loss of his railroad was a major financial setback, it did nothing to alter the respect and admiration people had for Banning and his influence remained steady. His Greek Revival-style house was the center for what Banning called "regales": parties that included senators, army generals, powerful businessmen, ship captains, and foreign ambassadors. This hobnobbing with the elite helped win him a seat in Sacramento as a State Senator, where he actively worked to build better transportation systems within the state.

After retiring due to poor health, Banning led a relatively peaceful life in Wilmington. He ran a few small businesses and traveled around the state. It was on one of these trips to San Francisco in 1884 when a wagon driver failed to see him in the street, knocked him down, and severely injured him. Banning died in his hotel room at the age of fifty-four and was buried in the Angeles-Rosedale Cemetery.

After his death, Banning's sons continued his business ventures and his youngest son, Hancock, maintained the mansion, living there until his death in 1894, after which various family members would reside in the house until it was purchased by the City of Los Angeles in 1925.

The Banning Mansion was built in the Greek Revival style once popular in the eastern United States, but out of style by the time of its completion. Over the years, the family added on rooms and two kitchens to the rear of the house, removed one wall so as to expand the "living" room, and removed several barns and outhouses on the property. Today, the house, one barn, and a small outer building are all that remain of the original ranch that is now operated as a museum by the City of Los Angeles.

Paranormal Activity

There are many reports of activity at Banning's magnificent house. Some of the tales are obvious urban legend with no basis in historical fact, such as the reports of "General" Banning being seen at a planning table with his officers devising battle strategy. This never would have occurred due to Banning being a General in name only; his title was purely ceremonial and he had no subordinates. All military matters would have been handled at Fort Drum, just to the south of Banning's home.

The museum is situated in a park surrounded by a residential neighborhood, and those residents in view of the mansion have reported seeing lights moving through the home in the dead of night, although it had been closed hours earlier. They have heard the sound of wagons moving up and down the long driveway... as if the ranch were still in its active days. Others have heard the sounds of laughter and merriment — as if one of Phineas's regales were in progress — and still others have seen the figure of a woman walking along the second-floor balcony and even Banning himself busy working in his first-floor office.

Although the docents have said they have never had the sense that the property was haunted, guests who have toured the house have reported smelling cigar smoke — as if the men of the house were socializing in the den — and caught the whiff of perfume in the parlor, where the women would gather. At other times, the sound of children in their bedroom and even muffled whispers have been heard coming from the closed-off third-floor servants' quarters.

Whether the Banning museum is actually haunted as residents and visitors believe or is just a product of urban legend being built up over a span of time and developed by locals on Halloween night, one thing is for sure: the Banning house is a place that every Angelino should visit, as well as all those interested in the history of the port. Its rare architectural beauty and Victorian furnishings make it one of the truly hidden treasures of Los Angeles. Just remember: When you visit, say hello to Phineas...for he was always one to make his guests feel welcome and it is always best to be polite to one's ghost host.

BANNING RESIDENCE MUSEUM

401 E. M Street	Visitor Information
Wilmington, CA 90744	Tours: Tuesday-Thursday: 12:30, 1:30, 2:30 p.m.;
310-548-7777	Saturday-Sunday: 12:30, 1:30, 2:30, 3:30 p.m.
www.thebanningmuseum.org	Office Hours: Monday-Friday, 9 a.m. to 4 p.m.

The Camarillo bell tower glows in the campus lights.

Camarillo State Hospital

In 1929, the state of California purchased a large, 1,500-acre parcel of land from the 8,600-acre Lewis Ranch, forty miles north of Los Angeles and three miles south of the town of Camarillo. The property, once part of the land grant known as Rancho Guadalasca, was by the 1920s owned by Joseph Lewis and Adolfo Camarillo, whose family the town was named after. The state paid just over $400,000 for the site that was to become California's most famous or, as some would say, infamous, hospital. Ground-breaking took place on August 15, 1933, and was attended by many dignitaries, including then-Governor James Rolph. The Federal Public Works Administration, which had been formed by President Roosevelt under his "New Deal" program, teamed up with the State of California for the three years it took to construct the hospital. On October 12, 1936, newly-elected Governor Frank Merriam dedicated Camarillo State Hospital, which opened its doors to the first of what would be thousands of patients.

The first complex consisted of a multi-acre central courtyard; a mission-style bell tower adorned a huge dining hall and its north-facing wall. The first official patients, adult men, were housed in this bell tower and then, in 1937, three hundred female patients who were being transferred from other, overcrowded hospitals came to Camarillo and a second complex was built to house them. These were dubbed the North and South complexes and were divided into male and female wards, the North being set aside for the females. As the need grew, so did the grounds of the facility. A labyrinthine two-story building was built just east of the two central complexes; this was the receiving and treatment building. The structure also housed the pharmacy, surgery rooms, admissions, and even the morgue. In 1947, a ward for the admission of children was opened. To the west, a series of structures were built for fire services, power generation, building maintenance, motor pool, and ambulance service, plus other various needs associated with the hospital.

The town of Camarillo at this time was quite rural and there were not many places for the 1,500 or so employees to live. To solve this problem, housing for the staff was built on the grounds of the institution itself; these were located about a half-mile away in a valley, which afforded the residents a bit of normalcy away from the hospital facility. Single-family homes were constructed for the administration and doctors and multi-unit buildings for the many nurses and other employees. These areas became a community for the people living there, complete with the problems, rumors, scandals, and alliances of any neighborhood in America.

Over the years, the hospital added to this community a pool, coffee shop, bowling alley, and even a TV studio. There was a large auditorium where dances were held and movies were shown. In the fields adjacent to the residence area, crops were planted and the patients would help plant and harvest the food for use at the hospital, with the extra produce sold to the locals in town. They even had their own dairy on the site.

In the early 1950s, construction began on a new Children's Unit complex. A section of land between the main complex and the residential area was chosen for this building and would include a dining room, playgrounds, swimming pool, and a school. This structure deviated from the Spanish appearance of the rest of the complex in that it was constructed using all red brick. The ward was finished and opened in 1955; in later years, an adolescent section was built with many of their own facilities, including a high school. However, in the waning years of the hospital, the adolescents would be housed in units in the bell tower.

The hospital was known as a leader in using new therapies and treatments; however, these may sometimes not have been the best course for the patient. For many years, lobotomies were performed, causing the patient damage that they could never recover from. Electroshock (ECT) therapy was used in the false belief that this could somehow "snap" the patient back to normalcy if applied enough times. These procedures were not only used for therapy, but also applied as punishment. Patients who caused disruption in the daily routine too often would be taken for "treatment" to the ECT room, where they would have the opportunity to "calm down." If the patient showed too many instances of erratic or violent behavior, then the "calming" procedure would be to lobotomize them. Because of this punitive approach, which became deemed as inhumane, and the advent of major tranquilizers, along with other medications, the state shut down all lobotomies and electroshock use at Camarillo by the early 1970s.

Shadow people, or Camarillo spirits, peering out from their wardroom.

Planet Paranormal team members devise a plan for their investigation.

I was a freshman at Channel Islands State and was living in the dorms when I heard about the so-called ghosts that were supposedly all over campus. Being from the Midwest (Kansas), I really didn't know that much about what the school had been before it became a college, but I was going to find out. I decided to do some research on the place and was amazed at the history of the school and its past incarnation. The more I read, the more I started to believe that the place might have indeed been haunted.

I began talking with other students who lived on campus, asking them whether or not they had any kind of paranormal events while at school. Many laughed at me and others seemed to just get funny looks on their faces and would walk away; then there were those that told stories ranging from seeing faces looking at them from empty windows to those saying they had objects thrown at them. All of these stories, whether true or not, got me interested in finding out for myself if any of them were true.

I decided that I would try to form an informal group to investigate the University to see if, in fact, there was any validity to the reports of ghosts occupying the buildings of this campus. It was surprisingly easy to form this group and we even had to put a few on a waiting list. We found out early on that the college itself did not want to have any part of our project and would not cooperate in the least, so at first we just went from building to building, looking in windows and hoping to find something looking out at us. This really didn't net any results and we were all beginning to get discouraged. It was then that my friend, Brandon, decided to look at other paranormal groups' web pages and see if he could find out better ways to investigate; with 20/20 hindsight, we found that we should have done this as our first thing…for we realized that everything we needed to learn was on these sites.

We began to buy some equipment that we discovered was essential to ghost hunting: voice recorders, digital cameras, and IR (infrared) video equipment. Armed with our new stuff, we resumed our investigation with new vigor. Slowly, we started to realize that we could hear voices on our recorders that were unfamiliar and started getting many orbs in pictures that we took facing the empty windows — it seemed at last we were starting to get some proof of activity at our school.

One night, as we were wandering around campus just north of the old bell tower, we discovered a door that was not locked — this was to an old abandoned building. We didn't know what the building used to be, but that didn't matter to us, as we had finally found an old, vacant area to search. We were a little nervous about being caught by security and being put on academic probation for violating the college's rules, but we couldn't help ourselves, and eagerly went into the structure. Once inside, we found ourselves in an old hospital ward area. There was what looked like an office area, a room that appeared to be a sort of lounge — whether for staff or patients I don't know — and even a few bathrooms. We looked around for a bit, recording any sounds or possible silent recording to hear later, and then wandered off down a long hallway.

The hallway we were following had several rooms on either side and a shower with three stalls on one side. It ended, we thought, in a double door; the door, however, led to another hall with more rooms, ending with a very large, long room, perpendicular to the corridor down which we had come. One member of our group, Christine, said that she was getting an odd feeling from this large room, so we decided to do a recording and snap a few photos. In just about every shot, we captured orbs and strange light anomalies coming from the windows. We entered this room and headed down to the opposite end and were just about to start recording again when we heard a noise from behind us (the direction back to the only door)...we all turned and there before us stood a woman dressed in what appeared to be a hospital gown. She just stared at us with a blank expression on her face, almost as if she wasn't sure she was actually seeing us here in the room. Beth was starting to hyperventilate, and I was almost about to scream when this woman opened her mouth — as if she were screaming — and then simply vanished. We all just stood there for a few moments, not knowing what to say, and then as one we all bolted for the door.

Once we had all gotten back to my dorm room, we calmed down and then we just started talking all at once. Yes, we all saw her vanish — and we all knew we had seen a real ghost. It is something none of us I'm sure will ever forget. We have never been on an investigation since and have all gone our separate ways after graduation, but one thing is for sure...I now know that the Channel Islands campus is indeed haunted.

~ Marco Ridgeway

Around 1967, the hospital began to admit patients who needed constant assistance to survive. These patients included those with mental retardation, autism, Down syndrome, and other brain disorders. The workshops created for the patients allowed them to be productive and the items they produced became highly prized by the locals in town. These patients were also involved with the Special Olympics program that became a great area of pride and accomplishment for not only the patients, but the staff, as well.

The hospital had, over the years, many suspicious deaths, and in 1976, authorities in Ventura County opened a Grand Jury investigation of Camarillo State Hospital. This resulted in quite a few indictments of staff members. Another result was that the state incorporated many new changes in the state hospital system, with its main focus on Camarillo. New procedures for patient restraint, medication, observation of suicidal patients, and safety procedures were but a few. Penalties were strengthened for employees who were too lax or too aggressive towards patients and investigations of complaints were conducted immediately upon the complaint being lodged.

The state hospitals were very expensive to operate and Camarillo was no exception. By the 1970s, the population at the hospital was on the decline and patients who were deemed able were being released into communities to try and lead normal lives. Many programs were being discontinued to save needed funds and whole sections of the complex were being shut down. The 1980s saw these cutbacks deepen as the state and federal budgets were scaled down, and by the 1990s, it became obvious that Camarillo could not survive. Rumors of its closure spread and, in May 1996, Governor Pete Wilson assigned a task force to investigate the possibility of closing the facility. The investigation concluded that the hospital, which once housed over 7,000 patients and now accommodated only around 800 and cost $114,000 per patient, should at the very least be scaled down. That was not to be, however, and on June 30, 1997, Camarillo shut its doors for good.

Over the years, many ideas were brought forth on what to do with the property. Because of the layout, the State decided that a prison would be the best use and plans were put forth to do the conversion; however, once the surrounding community heard about what the state was doing, the outrage and opposition was too much and the state abandoned the idea. Interest from the Cal State Universities was already known and this led to talks and the final conversion of the property. Today, with most of the original 1930s building being preserved, Cal State Channel Islands makes its home where the "Hotel California" used to be. It opened its doors in 2002 and became Ventura County's first public university.

Paranormal Activity

With so many disturbed and violent patients, along with the horrible treatment once thought therapeutic but now known as barbaric, and suicides, beatings, sexual assaults by patients, as well as a few murders and countless medical deaths, is it any wonder that Camarillo should be haunted? Over the years, many people have reported hearing the laughter of children and voices of the young playing. These occur in many areas around the campus, but most frequently in the area once designated as the children's ward. Apparitions have been glimpsed in many of the unoccupied rooms and corridors, objects moving with no explanation as to why, and EVPs caught in many places inside and out, but mostly the wards where patients were kept. There is even a road that seems to have more than its share of accidents leading into the back of the campus. People have photographed faces staring at them through windows in rooms that have been unoccupied for years, mists that move around the grounds and defy the direction of the wind, and even the smells of a hospital no longer in operation.

Planet Paranormal's investigations have caught many of the above phenomena, including a member getting a feeling of extreme anxiety to the point of near panic while in a building of the women's ward. As this member has never been prone to panic or feelings of discomfort on any previous investigation, we found this to be quite unusual.

The site is now a working State University with dorms on the campus itself, so if you decide to visit, please be respectful of the campus and the students who live here. The school police are quite active in patrolling and are very good at their job.

We consider this location to have moderate paranormal activity, but with that said, the history and architecture alone make any trip to this area worthwhile.

CAMARILLO STATE HOSPITAL

(California State University Channel Islands)
One University Drive
Camarillo, CA 93012

Casa de Estudillo main entrance.

Casa de Estudillo

The Casa de Estudillo, or The Estudillo House as it is also known, was built in 1827 by General Jose Maria Estudillo and later, after his death in 1830, completed by his son, Jose Antonio Estudillo. The adobe structure was erected in the style of the Spanish Dons that were prevalent at that time. The house is arranged in a "U" pattern with an outside covered corridor connecting the rooms, as well as each being linked in succession by an interior doorway.

The Estudillo family was one of the more influential families in San Diego at that time, with Jose Maria being the Presidio commandant and his son, Jose Antonio, holding numerous public offices. Their holdings were extensive and included Rancho Temecula, Rancho San Viejo near Hemet and Rancho San Jacinto, Jamal, Otay, and El Cajon. In addition to farming and owning wineries, the family raised cattle on most of the properties.

Sporting twelve rooms, Casa de Estudillo was quite large for its time. One of the rooms within the house was a private chapel; this was built not only for the family's use, but that of the other residents of Old Town as well. The priests would come down from the mission and perform mass and tend to the spiritual needs of the people. The Casa was used this way until the Chapel of the Immaculate Conception was built on Conde Street. The house was even used as a school for the local children, with one of the rooms being converted during the day to a classroom and being turned back into a parlor in the evening. The house was also a social hub for more than fifty years and was built to overlook the plaza of Old Town, where bullfights and other amusements and shows were held.

Jose Antonio died in 1852. His family continued to run the Casa until 1887, when they decided to move north to Los Angeles. By that time the book *Ramona* by Helen Hunt Jackson had caught the imagination of the entire country and people flocked to Southern California to see where the characters from the book worked, loved, and lived. Casa de Estudillo was thought to be where Ramona was married, although Jackson never visited the site. The *San Diego Union* perpetuated this in an article in 1887 that stated: "To sleepy Old Town the house is known as the Estudillo's. To the rest of the world, it is known as the marriage place of Ramona." The caretaker that was left in charge of the home when the family moved took full advantage of the *Ramona* furor and began selling off pieces of the house he had chipped off the walls to the tourists as souvenirs. Because of this, the building began to decay at an alarming rate.

This wholesale destruction continued for years and, as the opening of the new century dawned, Casa de Estudillo was nearing total ruin. In 1906, the property was sold by Jose Guadalupe and Salvador Estudillo to Nat Titus, who, in turn, sold it to John D. Spreckles, owner of the San Diego Electric Railway Co. and the *San Diego Union* newspaper, who had a business interest in obtaining the Casa. He had decided that with the popularity of the Jackson novel *Ramona*, in combination with his railroad for transportation and newspaper as advertisement, he would turn the whole area into one big tourist attraction with Casa de Estudillo as its anchor. Regardless of his reasons, his vision would be the salvation of the old house and, in turn, what we now know as Old Town, San Diego.

Spreckles hired architect Hazel Wood Waterman to restore the property to as close to the design mentioned in the novel as possible. Waterman was the protégée of noted San Diego architect Irving Gill and was quite up to the task. She hired local Mexican labor that painstakingly used the old methods of brick making and tile work to recreate the ambiance of the period while still keeping with the theme laid out in the novel. The original cupola atop the entryway was removed, as well as the balcony, because they were not mentioned in the book, and she designed the gardens in a much more elaborate fashion than would have been practicable for the Estudillos. Some of the changes included installing modern electric lighting and indoor plumbing and moving several doors and windows, but, in the end, she was able to restore the home to its former place of prominence.

After the completion of the restoration in 1910, Spreckles hired showman Tommy Getz to manage the property, which was marketed as a *Ramona*-themed tourist attraction. Getz plunged into his work and began to highly market the Casa and began to label all sorts of items with the moniker "Ramona's marriage place,"

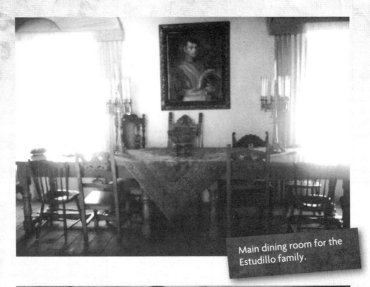

Main dining room for the Estudillo family.

The Estudillo family altar, also used for community church services.

I have lived just down Harney Street for many years and being so close to Old Towne have wandered around the square many times after eating at one of the restaurants. My girlfriend Darcy and I had just finished eating at the El Fandango and needed to work off our dinner, so we decided to take a stroll around the park. It was still early and we wandered into a few of the shops that were just closing up, enjoying each other's company. Coming out of the candy shop, Darcy noticed how pretty the old adobe, known as the Casa De Estudillo, was in the setting sun and asked if we could go over and walk around inside. Unfortunately, it was already closed and we couldn't get in, but Darcy still wanted to walk around the outside. She said that she always loved the place and just wanted to look in the windows and look at the rooms that she described as being so quaint.

We were going down the west side of the adobe when we started to hear music coming from one of the rooms. We glanced in a couple [of the windows] and couldn't see where the music would be coming from and decided that it was most likely coming from the Cosmopolitan Hotel that had just opened recently. Either way, Darcy was still looking into the rooms. We came to the last window in the row, and when Darcy looked in, she gave a big gasp and stumbled back a bit. I asked her what was wrong and she said it was nothing, that she had seen an old woman in the room and she had scared her because she hadn't expected anyone to be in any of the rooms. I thought it was strange that anyone would be in a dark, light-less room, but an old woman? I looked into the room myself and when I put my face up to the window... there was this old face, a woman's, staring back at me with a strange smile on her face. As I moved backwards, the face, which had been right up to the window, just vanished.

To this day, I am still not sure what it was that I saw. I believe it was the ghost of maybe the grandmother of the Estudillo children, but Darcy thinks I was just seeing the old lady back out of the window and leave the room.

~ Morris Acosta

as well as producing more postcards than any other *Ramona* attraction. The place even had a souvenir shop and restaurant. Due to this highly publicized association as the wedding place in the book, couples soon began to request holding their weddings there as well.

Getz purchased the property from Spreckles in 1924 and continued to operate the attraction successfully until his death in 1934, when his daughter, Marguerite Weiss, took over ownership. Weiss continued to operate the Casa for another thirty years, finally selling the home in 1964 to the Title Insurance and Trust Company. The company only held onto the Estudillo home for a short time before selling it to local businessman and philanthropist Legler Benbough, who, in turn, donated the entire property to the State of California in 1968.

The State Parks Service decided that the more historic aspect of the adobe should be highlighted rather than the fictional relationship with the Helen Hunt Jackson novel and set out to restore the structure to its original configuration, which included placing the cupola back over the entryway. As the State wanted to distance the place from the *Ramona* nomenclature, it removed any and all signs, brochures, and any reference to the book found on the property. No mention was ever given to the book's link to Casa de Estudillo and the State would not even acknowledge it until sometime in the 1990s. When the application for Historic status was submitted, it was filled out as Estudillo House/Ramona Marriage Place.

Paranormal Activity

No one knows why Casa de Estudillo is reportedly haunted. While it was home to the Estudillos, it knew only the joy of family and friends; yes, it did have some disappointment, but what home doesn't when life is lived within its walls? The Casa is a beautiful structure that also gives off a slightly creepy air with its shadowed rooms and corridors. Whether the house is haunted or not, the reports of activity are still being reported by guest and employee alike.

Some of the guests have reported cold spots appearing on even the hottest days; these cold areas can be so intense as to cause the hairs on the arm and nape of the neck to stand up. The faint sounds of prayer have been heard coming from the chapel room, as well as the pages of the Bible turning as if an unseen person is reading the "Good Book." Cameras have also been known to stop working, their batteries dead even though they were brand new.

There have been times when a guest would ask the docent if the bread they are smelling coming from the garden oven would be for sale so they could try it, only to find out that the oven has been unlit and unused for years. Music has also been heard emanating from one of the rooms. There have also been reports of flashing red lights appearing in the rooms and then mysteriously vanishing.

Some of the more frightening reports that have come out of La Casa are those of seeing actual apparitions. These come in the form of employees reporting faces appearing in the mirrors, and a little girl who likes to sit and sway back and forth

Casa de Estudillo gardens bathed in infrared light.

Planet Paranormal team members pose in the reflection of the case containing the Estudillo religious artifacts.

in a rocking chair. A figure that is believed to be one of the Padres who lived in the home has been seen gliding into the chapel, his brown robes trailing behind. A guest once said he heard a man yell for him to "get out," although there was no one else in the room with him at the time.

Perhaps the most memorable and most frightening occurrence took place many years ago in the garden. A couple had just gotten married and was having their picture taken next to the well. The bride glanced down and saw a disembodied pair of eyes looking back. The bride let out a terrified scream and fainted. Because of this the well has been filled with cement and no more reports have been made.

Planet Paranormal has conducted numerous daylight investigations of this location and have yet to capture any evidence of paranormal activity. That does not mean, however, the spirits of this graceful museum do not exist, but it is for this reason that we rate La Casa as having light paranormal activity.

Casa de Estudillo is a wonderful example of early California architecture and a great way to see how wealthy Mexican settlers lived and gave back to their community. It is also set right in the middle of one of the best State Historic Parks in California — Old Town San Diego. It is well worth a visit and one can easily spend the whole day exploring the area, shopping, and dining in the atmosphere of old Mexico.

CASA DE ESTUDILLO

Old Town SHP	Visitor Information
4002 Wallace Street	Casa de Estudillo is open 10 a.m. to 5 p.m. daily,
San Diego, CA 92110	free of charge.
619-220-5422	

Drum Barracks main entrance information display.

Drum Barracks

The Civil War. For many, this term is about the east coast of the United States. Places like Gettysburg, Appomattox, and Shiloh are where scores of Americans killed their brothers and fought for the rights they believed in. There are not many that know that California had an important role in the preservation of this nation and its freedom in the War Between the States.

Los Angeles had a large population of immigrants from southern slave states at the time the war broke out and Phineas Banning was concerned that this could cause the Union to lose the area, which would also mean the loss of the state itself. He sent a letter to President Lincoln with his concerns and the wheels were set in motion for what would become the lynch pin of the defense of California and the entire Southwest.

Though Fort Tejon had been the primary garrison at the time, authorities realized it was too far away from the growing port of New San Pedro. They initially set up a new camp in what is now Culver City, but soon realized that — at eighteen miles away — it was also too distant, so Banning and his partner, Benjamin D. Wilson, sold sixty acres of land to the U.S. Government, for $1 apiece, to be the site of the new fort.

Construction began on Camp San Pedro in 1862 and took a year to complete at a then unheard of cost of $1 million dollars. Even before work began on the camp, troops were sent down from Fort Tejon and Latham (near Culver City) to help set up the perimeter fencing and magazine stores. Later arrivals to Camp Drum, however, would remark on how it was the finest barracks they had ever seen and marveled at the hospital facilities that were erected for them. Banning, who thought it would be appropriate to honor the Assistant Adjutant General of the Army Colonel Richard Coulter Drum, recommended to the Governor that Camp San Pedro be renamed. The U.S. Army approved and Camp Drum became its new moniker. Over the next couple of years, all papers and documents were officially stamped as Drum Barracks and that name is the one we know it by today.

Drum Barracks became home to the California Column under the command of Colonel James Henry Carleton. This force was widely recognized as being one of the best equipped units in the army and, thus, one of its best fighting units. In 1862, after Texas volunteers fighting for the Confederacy overtook parts of New Mexico and Eastern Arizona, Carleton led his troops on the longest march of the Civil War, to fight its westernmost skirmish in what became known as the Battle of Picacho Pass.

In 1864, the troops of the camp were again called out to deprive the rebels of an anchorage by which they could raid ships carrying precious ores coming from the rich Comstock Lode. A company of the 4th California Infantry was sent to Catalina to set up a small garrison and ordered all non-military persons off of the island. They set up Camp Catalina Island on the Isthmus; what today we know as Two Harbors. The barracks are still standing and are now used by the Isthmus Yacht Club — they are the oldest structures on the island.

After the war, Drum was used as a staging area for troops heading to western territories where Native American attacks were taking place in what became known as the Indian Wars. It was the main depot for supplies and weapons for the entire West Coast. One of the more exotic experiments the army tried at that time can also be traced through Drum Barracks. I am speaking, of course, of the Camel Corps.

The camels were originally stationed at Fort Tejon, but when that unit was sent down to Los Angeles to help quell any secessionist ideas the camels came with them. Not having the appropriate facilities other than at Drum Barracks, that is where the dromedaries were stabled. The camels were tested to see if they could give the U.S. Army an edge in desert warfare over the horses used by the Confederate soldiers and Indians. It soon became clear, however, that the animals' temperaments were not suited to the American Southwest or the U.S. Cavalry.

The animals were kept at Drum Barracks for just under two years and in that time had virtually devastated the area's grasslands. They had been tested as military mounts, desert couriers, and even as pack animals, but every incarnation proved to be a failure. The post commander at that time sent a strongly-worded letter to Secretary of War Edwin Stanton, pleading with him to do something with the "ornery, spitting, foul tempered beasts." The camels were transferred and sold at auction, thus ending America's attempt at taming the "ships of the desert."

All that remains of the Drum Barracks today.

The only camel that still resides at the old fort.

Drum Barracks continued for only a couple years after the war and then it was decided that the cost of maintaining the base was greater than the return. As per the original contract, the land was given back to Banning and Wilson for the original $1 per acre; they also purchased at auction some of the buildings from the Army. For its investment of $1 million, the U.S. government got back just over $6,000.

Over the years, the property has been used for a number of different endeavors. B. D. Wilson opened a Methodist College that became so successful it was decided to move it closer to Los Angeles. Banning, who purchased the majority of the land, built a grand Victorian mansion and moved into the northern section of the camp, where he lived until his death. The junior officers' quarters were turned into a boarding house and as the years passed sections of the old fort were sold off to various oil companies and land-use agencies.

In 1927, Drum Barracks was designated a historic monument and, in 1931, it was officially declared California Historic Landmark #169. Even these prestigious designations could not stop time from slowly eating away at the structures made of wood and tin, which were left to the elements. By 1962, all but the old powder magazine and the now-uninhabitable junior officers' quarters remained and developers were chomping at the bit to raze these.

Walter Holstein formed the Society for the Preservation of Drum Barracks with the goal of saving the two structures that remained, but it would take five years of bureaucratic red tape for anything to be done and the old officers' building continued to deteriorate. In 1967, the State of California stepped in and purchased the property with the intent of transforming the structure into a Civil War museum.

The Preservation Society was given the task of refurbishing, maintaining, and operating Drum Barracks. It took years to fully develop and collect the needed artifacts for the museum, but, in 1986, the State turned over the property with the condition that it would always operate as a museum for the City of Los Angeles. It remains today in this capacity.

Paranormal Activity

Considering the history of Camp Drum, the state-of-the-art hospital that was there, and the fact that it served the area even after the camp closed, it should come as no surprise that the old building could be haunted. The conditions, even in a camp as well stocked as any of that time, during wartime would still have been hard. Many soldiers would have met their demise while engaged in their duties to this country and many may not be aware that they have passed into the spirit realm.

Over the years, visitors and docents alike have reported experiencing many unexplained occurrences at Drum Barracks. On a recent trip to the site, our guide told us that when she first started working there she would smell tobacco smoke in many of the rooms, as well as perfume. Smoking is strictly forbidden in the museum, so there would not be any residual smoke, and she said that each time she caught a whiff of a woman's perfume the building had been empty, save for her.

These admissions closely fit with reports that other people who have worked at the Drum Barracks have made. The docent also said that there were times she would lock up, but then turn back to the building and there would be lights on and locked doors open on the inside that she was certain she had taken care of before she left. Residents who live nearby have told of hearing the sound of chains rattling in the dead of night and horses clopping around as if the old camp were still in operation. Others have told of seeing figures moving inside and have heard talk coming from the closed and locked building.

As the Civil War progressed and it became clear that it would not spread to California or Camp Drum, the commanding officers became more lax with their rules regarding the families of the men stationed there. They would allow, on occasion, the wives and children to come live at the camp. It is believed that the child that is often heard playing in Drum Barracks is one such family member, as every now and then a guest or docent will hear the sound of a ball rolling down the stairs or bouncing in the hallway. When they go to investigate, there is no one there and no ball to be found. Psychics believe that it is the spirit of a young boy who may have died at the hospital some time in the late 1880s.

Apparitions have been seen wandering the rooms and hallways, many wearing the Union Army uniform. One such spirit is believed to be that of the camp's first commander, Colonel James Curtis. The Colonel is most often glimpsed in the parlor room, perhaps checking on the comfort of his junior officers. There is another man seen who appears to be confused… he shambles around dazed before vanishing.

Another resident spirit is that of a woman wearing a formal hoop skirt and is most likely the cause of the lavender and violet perfumes many people have smelled over the years. No one is quite sure who she is, but she is commonly referred to as Maria. Different psychics have claimed that she is Colonel Curtis's wife and others claim that she was the girlfriend of one of the other officers stationed there. Hopefully, someday we'll know for sure.

Planet Paranormal was able to catch what seemed to by zydeco music playing while our tour guide was speaking — this music only played briefly and only that one time. No other evidence was gathered while at this location and it is near impossible to do an organized investigation of the building due to the current director's views on the paranormal. It is hoped that this will change in the future. It is for this reason that we rate Drum Barracks as having light paranormal activity.

The Civil War was the most deadly and destructive war in the history of our country, and it was fought across the whole of our land, but only those battles with the names of famous generals are commonly known today. California was pivotal in the Yankees winning the war, as it deprived Johnny Reb of an important Pacific water port and funded four percent of the war effort. Drum Barracks is a wonderful place to explore this dark chapter in our nation's history and learn about the amazing men and women who fought and died so others could be free. While you are there, you may just get the opportunity to talk to one of the officers who were stationed there and learn from them what we are still trying to piece together today.

I got a friend that lives near the museum — he won't let me tell you his name, but I was over at his house one night and we were outside on the front porch just chilling, when we started to hear horses. Not just the hoof sounds, but that noise [neighing] they make with their mouth and snorting. It seemed kinda weird in the middle of the city to hear this, so we started trying to figure out where it was coming from. We walked down the street toward the Civil War place and it got louder. We thought maybe they were going to have a history show or something and brought horses in for it. That's when my friend told me that the place was supposed to have *spantos* (ghosts). We thought it might be fun to go find out if that's what we were hearing, so we walked down the road and onto the front grass of the museum. We could still hear the horses, but now we thought we could hear people talking too. It was the sound of a lot of guys talking as if they were busy working. We could tell that it seemed to be coming from behind the building, so we looked over the fence, but didn't see anyone. Even though there was no one to see, we could still hear all of the talking and animals and stuff. It sounded like there were a whole bunch of people there and still there was no one there. We kinda stood there for a couple minutes and then walked back to his house. Our other friends think it's cool that we got to [hear] these *spantos* even if we couldn't see them.

~ Sergio Grajeda

DRUM BARRACKS

1052 Banning Boulevard
Wilmington, CA 90744
310-548-7509
www.drumbarracks.org

Visitor Information
Tours: Tuesday-Thursday, 10:00 to 11:30 a.m.;
Saturday-Sunday, 11:30 a.m. to 1 p.m.

One of the many artillery pieces that helped protect our Pacific Coast.

Fort MacArthur Museum

In 1888, President Grover Cleveland signed the executive order designating an area overlooking San Pedro Bay as a military site to help in the defense of the growing Los Angeles harbor. It wasn't until 1914 and after additional land had been purchased that the area was developed. The fort was divided into three parts: the Lower Reservation, Middle Reservation, and Upper Reservation.

The fort was named in honor of Lieutenant General Arthur MacArthur, Civil War Medal of Honor recipient and father of General Douglas MacArthur. The construction was completed by 1919, with the main armament placed on the Upper Reservation, battery Osgood/Farley, and battery Merriam/Leary. Each of these batteries contained two 14" guns mounted on disappearing carriages that could fire up to fourteen miles; along with these two long-range guns, a third battery, Barlow/Saxton, was constructed that contained 12" mortars housed in massive concrete emplacements. The armament for the Lower Reservation consisted of electronically-controlled mines ready for rapid deployment and four 3" rapid-fire cannons placed on Terminal Island to protect against enemy mine sweepers. The Middle Reservation would house the barracks and administration buildings.

World War I hastened the construction of the defenses and the flats of the Lower Reservation became a training center for troops headed for the front lines in Europe.

At one time, up to 4,500 soldiers were stationed at the fort during the war. The first regular troops to be posted at Fort MacArthur were the 38th artillery unit from Fort Scott, the 1st Coast Artillery Company, and various California National Guard units. A 23-bed hospital was built on the Middle Reservation, along with additional housing and office buildings.

After the war, the fort was used extensively as a training base for the National Guard and Coast Field defense units; Civilian Conservation Corps and Civilian Military Training Corps also used the base. It soon became apparent that the guns were becoming obsolete. As San Pedro became home to the Pacific Battle Fleet, the need to upgrade the defenses to longer-range cannon became a primary concern. As early as 1924, Brigadier General Harry Todd, who commanded the 9th Coastal Artillery, noted that the guns at Fort MacArthur were "too few and too short range to fulfill the mission of defense of the harbor." In 1930, two modern 14" railroad guns were installed on the Middle Reservation and given the name Battery Irwin and anti-aircraft guns were installed around all vulnerable sites. The new mobile guns could fire a 1,400-pound shell twenty-seven miles and were eventually stored in special buildings that allowed for rapid deployment. The test firings of these guns became a political issue due to damage to surrounding houses that ignored the warnings and the posted precautionary measures. It became such a hot topic that the War Department forbade any further firing of the guns.

In February 1941, the first 1,000 draftees arrived at Fort MacArthur to news crews eager to film newsreel footage of the event; in September of that year, the first sentry dog unit of the K-9 Company was established at Fort MacArthur. Extensive advertising had gone out through the newspapers and dog owners had been told to bring likely candidates to Pershing Square in downtown Los Angeles. There the army chose the best dogs for training under Sgt. Robert Pearce. These were the first of what would become the internationally famous K-9 Command of the U.S. Army.

On December 7, 1941, the strength of the fort was 2,032 officers and enlisted men. When the call came in at 11:35 a.m. that morning, commanding officer Colonel Hicks immediately ordered all fortifications manned and all weapons and units to their selected positions and ammunition distributed to all. Communication with civil authorities and local law enforcement were established and throughout the rest of the day and into the next every report of Japanese ships and planes was relayed to gun crews, which then scanned the skies and the coast for eminent threats.

In the early months following the attack, Fort MacArthur remained on high alert. The freighter *Absoroka* was torpedoed off Point Ferman, but was able to limp into port and the *SS Montebello* was fired on and sank off the coast of San Simeon. The day following the torpedoing of the *Absoroka*, Battery F, 105th Field Artillery Battalion fired ten rounds at what was believed to be a submarine off the coast of Redondo Beach — it was believed to be the boat that had fired on the *Absoroka* and was presumed sank by the MacArthur unit.

Because of the slow rate of fire of the Battery Osgood/Farley and Merriam/Leary 14" guns and the short range and ineffectiveness against ships of the 12"

Fort MacArthur's upper reservation was a key defense point for the Los Angeles harbor.

The K-9 Corps had its start right at Fort MacArthur and many of its furry heroes are buried here with honor.

Legend says that comrades in arms still help guard the fort even today.

This was the second year my family had gone to Fort MacArthur Museum for their annual Fort MacArthur Day's celebrations. My three sons and I are able to see, sense, and communicate with spirits and I have learned from going to historical reenactments that places — normally quiet as a rule — tend to get more spirit activity during public events and Fort MacArthur is no exception. Cannon and gunfire are fantastic triggers for paranormal activity and I noticed this the first year we were at FM Day's, but we couldn't access the armory or barracks during the event.

During our 2010 visit the doors to the armory were locked, so we couldn't go inside. Even though the gates were locked, my twin boys could still see men in uniform walking around inside. I saw them too, but didn't want to draw unwanted attention to us. This was around 3:30 p.m. and I was really looking forward to getting into these rooms at another time. On our 2011 visit, however, we were able to access the armory. This year people were wandering in and out at will, as there was no attendant at the gate. I sensed at least one young male spirit inside, but didn't remind the boys of the ghost sighting from the year before. We took pictures in front of some of the weapons before heading into the long tunnel that connects the two sides of the armory.

Heading into the tunnel, I took the lead with my twins and eldest son behind and my husband further still taking pictures of the various exhibits. Due to its length, the middle is pitch-black with light only in the first ten feet at the beginning and end. I stayed close to my boys until I heard the young male spirit talking to me. I couldn't hear what he was saying besides "My name is…" because my kids were talking so loudly in the tunnel at that point. I whispered back to the spirit, "Hey, want to have some fun? Take my boys' hands like your me." I then lengthened my stride and told my sons, "Take my hand if you can't see." My boys came out of the tunnel with a surprised look on their faces and one twin said, "How did you get so far ahead of us?" The other twin said, "I thought I was holding your hand?" By this time, the spirit of the young man was standing next to me and I said, "What if I told you that you were holding hands with a nice young soldier ghost?" My boys said almost in unison, "Oh, mom, that's gross! Why did you make us hold a dead guy's hand?" I just laughed and so did the young soldier; I never did get his name, but I think he'll remember us the next time around.

~ Cornelia Heun-Davidson

mortars of Battery Barlow/Saxton, it had already been decided that upgraded 16" guns would be installed at Whites Point, a mile west of the Upper Reservation. Work began in 1943 and was completed shortly thereafter.

As the United States began pushing the Japanese naval forces back to their homeland, the need for all of the armament at Fort MacArthur lessened and in 1943, shortly after Whites Point was completed, the 12" mortars of Battery Barlow/Saxton were deactivated. In January of the following year, Battery Osgood/Farley and Merriam/Leary were retired as well. This left the two railway guns and the Whites Point reservation (Battery Paul D. Bunker) as the only shore guns protecting the Port of Los Angeles. As the Japanese were no longer capable of mounting a threat to the West Coast, they were more than enough to do the job.

Just prior to the end of WWII, Fort MacArthur became a separation station for the U.S. Army. Some of the 750,000 men who had gone to war through the fort now arrived back to a much happier situation. On April 16, 1946, the separation center was closed, having repatriated 150,710 men. Sergeant Howard McIntosh was the last to go home through its doors.

Beginning with the 12" mortars in 1943 and ending with the 16" guns of the Whites Point reservation being sold for scrap in 1946, all of the major coast artillery from Fort Mac was removed. By 1948, the staff of the fort dropped to three hundred troops and were tasked mainly with the maintenance of the anti-aircraft and mobile batteries. The fort also continued as an induction and separation center until 1950.

In the early 1950s, Fort MacArthur was converted to a Nike missile command and control center. The missiles were installed around the area, including Whites Point, Point Vicente, Torrance, Redondo Beach, and Malibu, along with cities more inland — all controlled from Fort MacArthur. However, by 1974, the Nike missile was obsolete and the Army again began to reduce its presence around the San Pedro area. By 1982, the base was officially turned over to the Air Force, which would use it for military housing; at the same time, the Upper Reservation was closed and most of the land was turned over to the Los Angeles School District, which still utilizes the site today. Battery Osgood/Farley and Merriam/Leary were given over as a museum.

Paranormal Activity

Over the years, there have been many reports of paranormal activity in and around Fort MacArthur. All of these seem to come from the visitors and tourists that flock to the museum. The curator and employees of the fort tend to dispute these claims as just coming from imagination and from the fact that an urban legend has sprouted up from many local teens in the area. One of these is that an explosion of one of the 14" guns killed "numerous" soldiers and that their restless spirits walk the tunnel where they were killed. I could find no record of this ever happening and the museum staff told me that the closest incident to this happened at Bluff Park, down the coast, and that only one man was killed and one injured. This legend was expanded on by the Cartoon Network when the show *Othersiders* reported hearing the men in the access tunnel. This is not to say that there is no activity at the fort. Reports of hearing footsteps and feeling cold breezes as if someone has passed close by have been told often. The sound of long-disused and inoperable machinery clanking to life has been heard and strange lights have been seen floating down dark and abandoned hallways. It is believed that the ghosts of long-dead servicemen are still going about the business of manning the fort. Only two men were known to have died at this section of Fort MacArthur — a soldier who committed suicide and a contractor killed in an industrial accident — so who the other spirits are is anyone's guess. We consider this site to have very mild activity.

For those of you who want to see a piece of California and American history, Fort MacArthur is the place. Who knows, you may just be the one to discover who is really looking after the fort and why they can't seem to leave.

FORT MACARTHUR MUSEUM

3601 S. Gaffey Street
San Pedro, CA 90731
310-548-2631
www.ftmac.org

The majestic *Queen Mary* stands tall under the lights of the harbor.

Queen Mary

The keel for the *Queen Mary* was laid down on January 31, 1931. She was to be the largest, at just over 1,000 feet and 81,000 tons, and the grandest ship afloat. Known at the time only as job #534 at the John Brown & Co. Ltd. shipyard, the construction on the replacement for the *Mauritania* was scheduled to be launched in May of 1932. However, due to the world economic depression hitting the shipbuilding industry extremely hard, Cunard announced that work was to be suspended on December 11, 1931. Over the next couple of years, Cunard tried to secure funding to continue building the ship, but was unable to and finally had to turn to the government for help. In 1934, an agreement was reached that required Cunard to buyout its chief rival, White Star Line, thereby forming Cunard White Star Ltd. Work again began in April of that year and was completed by August.

When job #534 was envisioned, it was agreed to name the ship "Queen Victoria." However, while visiting the palace shortly before completion, the King of England asked the chief designer what the name of the ship was to be and the response was, "We shall name her after the greatest Queen of our empire." Beaming, the King thanked him for the compliment, and said, "My wife would be honored to have the ship named for her." So it was that on September 26, 1934, the *Queen Mary* was christened by her namesake and launched into history.

It took only twenty months for the superstructure and outfitting to be complete and in March 1936 she sailed out of Clyde Bank and proceeded with her sea trials. She was handed over to Cunard White Star Ltd. on May 11, 1936 — and she was every bit as luxurious as she was said to be. She had three classes of accommodations: 3rd class in the bow of the ship, 2nd or tourist class to the aft, and 1st class in the center, also known as the smoothest sections of the ship. She had two swimming pools, three nurseries, and elevators in the bow, aft, and amidships, as well as salons and entertainment for all three classes of passengers.

On May 27, 1936, her massive 160,000 SHP engines grinding away, the grand ship headed out on her maiden voyage. Her four screws being able to produce 30 knots of speed led people to believe the ship would try to win the coveted Blue Riband, the award for the fastest crossing of the Atlantic from the *Queen Mary's* chief rival, the French liner *Normandie*. Thick fog en route to New York dashed any hope of this happening and the *Queen Mary* quietly sailed past the Statue of Liberty to safely deliver her passengers to the pier a few days later. However, after returning to England for a brief stay in dry dock for minor adjustments, her next voyage produced a maritime speed record and captured the trophy from the French. By May of 1937, the *Queen Mary* had carried just fewer than 57,000 passengers in one year's time.

In 1938, the *Queen Mary* won back the Blue Riband from the *Normandie* and set speed records for both the westbound and eastbound voyages. On September 3, 1939, she docked in New York Harbor just two days after Hitler invaded Poland to begin World War II. The *Queen Mary* would sit for six months while London decided what role she would play in the coming war.

It was decided that the best task for the *Queen Mary* would be as a troop transport. Joined in New York by her younger sister ship, the *Queen Elizabeth*, she underwent a conversion to wartime specifications: anti-aircraft guns were installed on her decks and her furnishings were removed, replaced by bunk beds and hammocks; medical stations were installed on her promenade deck and her three dining rooms were converted to mess halls and hospital areas; and her sleek, black-and-white-paint scheme was replaced by a dull gray, designed to camouflage her from patrolling aircraft and prowling U-boats. Even with the guns and camouflage, speed was still to be her greatest weapon and staunchest ally. She sailed from Sydney to her home port of Clyde, carrying Australian troops, and then back to Singapore and India. For the rest of 1940, the *Queen Mary* sailed between Australia and India, bolstering the defenses of that region.

When it became obvious Japan was on the move and the region became unsafe for shipping, it was decided to move the ship to Boston to undergo upgrades to her defenses. After America entered the war, the need to get U.S. troops to Europe became paramount and so the *Queen Mary* became a transport for the American military. In August 1942, she began her eastbound voyages, ferrying 10,000 to 15,000 U.S. servicemen to England. The *Queen Mary* still holds the record of having over 16,000 people aboard on one crossing. After the ship reached her port in Europe, she would be loaded with German and Italian prisoners of war for the return

One can almost hear the shoppers as they stroll down "Piccadilly Circus" on the *Queen Mary's* promenade deck.

The little girl in the mirror was not in the room when this photo was taken. Could this be our Jackie? *Photo courtesy of Jamie Dwyer (East Valley Paranormal)*

trip. At first, these prisoners were kept far below the water line in the forward cargo hold, but as the war progressed the prisoners were allowed to roam the upper decks as long as they behaved themselves.

It was on one of the eastbound legs of her journey that one of the worst tragedies of the *Queen Mary's* sailing career occurred. During the war, she was always escorted by naval war ships; these ships, although powerful, could not match the speed of the giant luxury liner. Because the U-boat threat was great in the Atlantic, the convoys were ordered to sail in a zigzag pattern to make it more difficult to aim torpedoes. It was on October 2, 1942, that the *Queen Mary* was steaming at 29 knots when the *HMS Curacao*, either not knowing the ship's pattern or just mistakenly too close to the giant liner, passed in front of her. Unable to stop in time, the *Queen Mary* sliced her escort in half: 329 British sailors lost their lives as the liner passed. Even if the ship could have stopped, she was under orders not to slow for any reason — the many troops she carried were too important to become targets for the German submarines lurking nearby. Upon entering the harbor, the liner's bow was patched with tons of cement and then she headed to Boston for more permanent repairs. After one more troop cruise around Cape Town to the Middle East and Australia, she returned to New York and spent the remainder of the war ferrying U.S. troops to and from European battlefields.

During the war, Adolph Hitler considered the *Queen Mary* to be a significant threat to his war effort, so he put a bounty on the liner. To any U-boat captain who sank her would be given $250,000 and the Order of the Iron Cross, the highest decoration Germany awarded. Because of this, the *Queen Mary* became a much-sought after prize; many a German sailor would spot her steaming at sea, only to watch her sail away at a speed they could not match. It was this ability, along with her gray paint scheme, that both nations began to call her "The Gray Ghost." In all, the ship traveled 600,000 nautical miles and transported 800,000 people.

After the war, one of the more pleasant tasks the ship had ever undertaken was when the "Bride and Baby" voyages began. In 1946, the *Queen Mary* transported 22,000 war brides and their children from Europe to Canada and the U.S. It also made numerous trips repatriating Canadian servicemen to Halifax.

The *Queen Mary* was officially transferred back to Cunard on September 27, 1947. After a ten-month refit back to liner service, she began weekly service from Southampton, Cherbourg, and New York. In January 1949, she ran aground outside of Cherbourg. Not wanting to wait for the ship to be freed, many of the passengers decided to make their way to Paris and fly to New York instead. This was to be an omen of things to come, as air travel was becoming more popular with the elite. Although she was still capable of making fast Atlantic voyages, the new American liner, the *United States*, captured the Blue Riband in July 1952 with an average speed of 35 knots. The *Queen Mary* would never recapture the prize.

In 1958, the ship was fitted with stabilizers, but already the future of the ship was in question. She began to make periodic cruises to the Canary Islands and the Bahamas, but without central air-conditioning or outdoor pools she was unsuited for that type of cruising. In May of 1965, a strike by the seamen's union cost the

Cunard line millions of dollars and spelled the end of the great ship's career. After more than 1,000 transatlantic crossings, the *Queen Mary* made her last scheduled crossing of the Atlantic on September 16, 1967. The ship was put up for sale and the bids began to roll in.

The City of Long Beach, California, was the highest bidder at $3.45 million, just beating out China in the bidding war. China planned to sail the ship to Hong Kong, where it would have been sold for scrap. The City of Long Beach had grander plans for the magnificent ship: she would become a world-renowned hotel, museum, and tourist attraction.

To help recoup some of the money lost from her last few voyages, Cunard decided to make her crossing to Long Beach a grand farewell event with port calls in Lisbon, Las Palmas, Rio de Janeiro, Valparaiso, Callao, Balboa, and Acapulco, and then, finally, Long Beach. The *Queen Mary* left England on October 31, 1967, and arrived in Long Beach on December 9th to much fanfare and celebration; after dropping her passengers safely once more at the dock, she then settled into her permanent mooring in an isolated corner of the Long Beach Harbor.

During her sailing days as a luxury liner, the *Queen Mary* played host to some of the world's most famous stars, royalty, and the well-known of the time. These included Cary Grant, Greta Garbo, Fred Astaire, the Duke and Duchess of York, David Niven, George and Ira Gershwin, Mary Pickford, Clark Gable, Alfred Hitchcock, Jimmy Durante, Bob Hope, and Oliver Hardy, to name a few. Winston Churchill sailed on her many times and had an office on her promenade deck during the war and is said to have signed the orders for the invasion of Normandy on the desk that is still in the suite that bears his name.

The transformation to a tourist attraction actually began in 1969, but due to financial woes and the sale of the parent company of the leaseholder, the ship's opening was delayed until May of 1971. By that time the ship had been gutted from "R" deck and below, the ship's boilers, forward engine room, generator rooms, and stabilizers had all been removed. The aft engine room and shaft alley would be spared to use as part of the museum. Because of a dispute between rival unions, the Coast Guard had to make a determination on the ship and ruled that, because of the fact she would never be able to sail again, she was deemed to be a building. This also took responsibility away from them and squarely on the city's fire department.

The promenade deck's starboard side was enclosed and transformed into two restaurants; her main lounges and dining rooms were turned into for-rent banquet facilities, and the famed observation bar was redecorated as a western-themed bar. The rooms on A and B decks would become the initial 150 hotel rooms while the smaller 1st class rooms, such as the library, lecture room, drawing room, and music room, would be turned over to retail space. Two more areas on the sun deck would be changed to retail and various spaces would be converted to concessions. These areas were once the most expensive of the first-class suites.

On the sun deck, the exclusive Veranda Grill would be gutted and converted into a hamburger and hot dog stand, the second- and third-class dining rooms

The 1ˢᵗ class pool as it appears today. *Photo courtesy of Dave Twolan @ www.flickr.com/photos/26860638@N08/*

Peter James — may he rest in love and light! *Photo courtesy of Tuesday Miles.*

converted into storage areas, and the Turkish baths, also on the R deck, would be removed. The second-class "bathing pool" would be converted into the Royal Theater, while the first-class pool would be used for hotel guests.

In May of 1971, the *Queen Mary* opened as a tourist attraction; however, the hotel had not yet been completed, so many of the sections on the ship remained closed to the public. The ship was initially only open weekends, but when Jacques Cousteau's Museum of the Sea opened the days expanded to include weekdays. Due to low-ticket sales, though, Cousteau's museum closed a few years later.

Hyatt operated the hotel from 1974 to 1980, after which the Jack Wrather Corp. signed a 66-year lease with the city. This company was taken over by the Disney Corporation in 1988. Disney bought Wrather as a way to gain ownership of the Disneyland Hotel and, therefore, paid only scant attention to the operations of the *Queen Mary*, which struggled during the years Disney owned the lease. Although they did have plans to build a theme park on the land surrounding the ship, Disney decided to develop DisneySea in Japan instead and even built a centerpiece for the park resembling the grand ocean liner. Disney gave up the lease in 1992 and the *Queen Mary* closed her doors to the public two months later.

The ship was closed for a year with the only visitors being the security guarding the ship. In February of 1993, the RMS foundation signed a five-year lease with Long Beach and the tourist areas of the ship opened back up later that month. The hotel would not reopen until March of that year; then, in 1995, the lease was extended to twenty years. That same year, Queens Seaport Development Inc. signed a 66-year agreement to control the land adjacent to the ship. Things looked good for the ship until 2005 when, due to a rent dispute with the City of Long Beach, QSDI filed for bankruptcy. The court requested bids for the lease in 2006 and a group called "Save the Queen" won the bidding for $41 million. They, like so many others before, plan to refurbish the ship and build a "city walk"-style resort shared with Carnival Cruise Lines that will include a marina, hotels, restaurants, and retail space.

Today, the *Queen Mary* is listed on the National Register of Historic Places and is the last remaining example of a pre-WWII transatlantic liner in existence. Her grace and beauty, although marred by the short-sightedness of those who sought to "transform" her into their idea of a museum, is still much in evidence. The Art Deco decor of her interior calls one to an era past, where things were at once simpler and more complex, a time when giants prowled the sea and mankind rode those giants. I believe it is for these reasons that the *Queen Mary* remains home to many of her past guests, those who, although dead, still remember their time aboard this grand lady of the sea.

Paranormal Activity

For many years, researchers in the paranormal field have been coming to the *Queen Mary* to seek out her resident ghosts. She is considered by many to be the most haunted ship afloat and possibly even the most haunted site in America. Some of the reports range from knocking sounds to seeing full-body apparitions. There are areas below the guest decks that insiders know to be hot spots and the first-class pool is said to have a "vortex" that allows spirits to pass between dimensions. This is not to say the decks that guests are allowed to roam do not have their fair share of paranormal activity…for on the *Queen Mary*, ghosts have and will appear at any time of day and anywhere on the ship.

The engine room around watertight door #13 is one of the most well-known haunts of the ship. Here, it is said that eighteen-year-old John Pedder, a crewman crushed by the door in 1966, is said to talk in low tones, knock on the bulkheads, and even appear to unsuspecting guests wearing blue overalls and walking the passageway before vanishing. There have been two men killed at this door; one by accident, one by murder. The propeller box just aft of door 13 is another spot that is said to be active. Here, the voice of a male is heard giving orders to unseen crewmen. It is thought to be one of the past captains who has come back to make sure the ship is cared for. The isolation ward at the far aft section is another hot spot for activity.

Up on the promenade deck, a man in an officer's uniform has been seen walking the deck, but when approached…he vanishes. The man is thought to be that of an officer who inadvertently drank tetra-hydra-chloride thinking it was gin. "The Queen's Salon," also on the promenade deck, has had reports of a beautiful woman dancing the night away; again, when she is approached, she vanishes. Officers have been seen on the bridge, in the radio room, and in various spots on the sports and command decks going about their duties as if they were still alive.

One area of the ship that is off limits to guests is the "Green Room." This is a small room set in one of the now empty generator rooms between boiler rooms. It was once used for performers to relax and compose themselves before going on stage. Here, it is said strange knocking sounds, voices, and the sounds of men working can be heard. In the ceiling of this room is a small hole in which people have said a male face will appear. The name associated with this spirit is thought to be John Henry, a crewman who was burned to death in the area.

World-renowned psychic Peter James spent countless hours researching the ship, and many of the spirits and their names come from his work. Two areas of the ship that are well-known come from James's ability to connect with the dead. These are the first- and second-class pools. The second-class pool is no longer on the ship, having been converted to the Royal Theater; however, the first-class pool is said to be the "heart" of the ship. It was here that Peter James, on film, had a conversation with the spirit of a little girl whose name, according to James, is Jackie. James first found Jackie in the Royal Theater; not knowing that the room used to be a pool, James was confused when the little girl told him to meet her in the other

We have stayed at the Queen Mary Hotel several times and have experienced many unexplainable events in our room. One morning we were getting dressed and heading out for breakfast. I was looking out one of the two portholes, taking pictures of Long Beach Harbor, and Vici was just finishing up in the shower and getting ready to step out of the tub when the bathroom door flew open. It did not open slowly — it *flew* open and smacked the wall really hard. Vici asked if I had done this and I said, "No, I was taking pictures out the window." We tried to debunk this by gently closing the door without latching it, but the door would not open on its own.

During another trip we were attending a paranormal event on the ship. We were told that when we made our reservations that we could request a haunted room, so we did. Upon checking in, we asked the person at the front desk if this was a haunted room; they said "yes" and told us what had been reported. We then got our keys and went to our room. We decided to rest for a bit before we walked around the ship. [While heading to our room] the light in the hallway turned off and then back on, but we didn't think much about it until it happened again; we looked at each other and smiled. After resting, we decided to go topside and take a walk. I turned off the TV and headed for the door. When we got to the door, the TV turned back on — these were the same reports the person at the front desk had told us about. Was this just a coincidence?

After leaving the room, we were walking down the long hallway to the main staircase. If you are familiar with the guest rooms on the ship, most of the guestroom doors are recessed down a short hallway. I was approaching one of these recessed hallways and saw a shadow of a person on the carpet…as if they were coming out of their room out to the main hallway. I stopped so I wouldn't walk into them, but no one stepped out. I looked down the hall and no one was there…the shadow disappeared as it came around the corner.

~ Joe and Vici Ruffulo

pool. After finding out that there was another pool, James and his escort hurried there — and what transpired there was history in the making. This incident helped propel James into the spotlight and helped land him his recurring appearances on the hit show *Sightings*.

Another area that is off limits, but is known to have high paranormal activity, is the forward cargo hold. This area was used to house German and Italian prisoners of war and the conditions were so deplorable that many died during the crossing. It is also very close to the area where the ship struck the *HMS Curacao*. Here people have heard voices speaking in German, Italian, and English. The sounds of metal being torn and the loud crash of impact have also been reported.

The reports of room B340 are a gimmick made up by the Disney Corp. to help sell tickets. This is not to say that you are safe from activity in the staterooms. Many reports from all over the hotel attest to the fact that the ghosts enjoy the comforts of the ship just as much as the worldly guests do. The reports are too numerous to mention here, but one room should be noted: B474. This room was the idea behind Disney's B340. A murder took place in this room and many people who stay here have given reports of things moving on their own, unexplained noises, doors opening and closing, and even voices.

Planet Paranormal has had the rare and fortunate privilege to have had almost unlimited access to the ship before Save the Queen assumed the lease. It was during this time that we gained some of the most profound evidence our group has been able to capture.

In the boiler room/green room area, we have captured EVPs of a male voice, audio of what sounds like a wrench or hammer striking metal, a little girl's singing, and a woman speaking. Although it is already dark in that section of the ship, there have been times when the depth of the darkness has gone to a level we could not explain. At other times members have reported seeing lights blink in the darkness above where there are no fixtures.

In the Royal Theater, members have seen the shadow of a spectral cat creeping down the aisles. This same cat, or there could be two, has also been seen in the first-class pool changing room. Also in the theater, a little girl has made herself known.

The cargo hold is one of the most haunted sites on the ship. It is thought that it might be the most haunted. Here members have actually heard disembodied voices talking about them being there. Voices asking each other, "What are they doing here?" and "What do they want?" Our members have heard conversations taking place all around them knowing they were the only ones in the small area. Planet Paranormal has also picked up a female voice in this area thought to be a nurse still caring for her charges. Directly above the cargo hold is a room that was used as a morgue during the war, which may account for some of the activity in this room. EVPs captured here have been in German and English.

By far the most famous and, for our investigators, the most beloved area of the ship is the first-class pool. The range of activity caught here is phenomenal. The changing room area is said to have a "vortex" in it and, if the activity in this area is any indication, then there is no argument. We have heard singing, laughter, growling, and screaming. In fact, Planet Paranormal appears to be the first to document an entity we call "Grumpy." His identity is unknown; however, he does like to make himself the center of attention. Grumpy has been known to wander the ship, yet he seems to prefer the pool area. He has been known to growl in people's ears, although he can sometimes be heard from afar as well. One of the things he likes to do is get a person isolated and then get very close to their ear and give a deep guttural growl. I have personal experience with this, as Grumpy, with this tactic, was the first to get me to understand that there was something on the other side.

Sarah is another girl said to frequent this area and seems to have appointed herself guardian of the other, younger girl, Jackie. Our investigators have many EVPs of Sarah, as well as hearing her singing to, we assume, Jackie. However, it is Jackie who has stolen our hearts.

Robert Davis, owner of Planet Paranormal Radio and founder of Planet Paranormal, seems to have a rapport with this little girl that rivals, if not exceeds that of Peter James. While participating at a paranormal event on the ship in 2007, there was a mass investigation of the pool area in which the lights were turned off. Jackie does not like change and was apparently scared. When we entered the pool, this little girl sought out Bob and actually gripped his hand — this sent a wave of her fear through him to the point that he had to leave the area. A year later, at the same event, Bob Davis and myself would record Jackie on two different devices speaking to us for over fifteen minutes. This audio has been analyzed and is almost a perfect match for the voice captured by Peter James twenty years earlier. To this day, we can simply walk through the pool, say "Hi Jackie, just passing through," and she will answer back with a cheerful "okay." This has been witnessed by at least one security guard who was escorting us with humorous consequences.

Planet Paranormal considers this site to have extremely high paranormal activity. Many of the places off limits to guests are accessible by taking one of the great paranormal tours available Thursday through Sunday nights; they will even allow you to book your own investigation. Even if you decide not to take one of these tours, you can still wander the ship by taking the self-guided tour. This allows you to go to all of the common areas of the ship, including the engine room, isolation ward, promenade, bridge, and all upper decks. If you decide to rent a room, you will be able to do all of the above, plus access some of the lower hotel areas.

The *Queen Mary* is a treasure that can be savored by anyone willing to seek life as it used to be, when grand liners ruled the waves and big bands ruled the stage, so if the thought of seeing beautiful Art Deco bas relief woods and furnishings is appealing or dining in one of her fine restaurants beckons to you, then come to the magnificent *Queen Mary* and become part of her history. Once you do, she will get under your skin and you will come back again and again.

1126 Queens Highway
Long Beach, CA 90802
562-435-3511
www.queenmary.com

Visitor Information

The Queen Mary Hotel is open daily, 10 a.m. to 5 p.m.

Rates: Rates vary by room and accommodations. Suites also vary by size. There is a $15 a day charge for parking. Package deals are available. Check-in is 4 p.m. and check-out is noon. Attraction prices are:

- For 1st class admission: $32.95 for adults, $28.95 for Military and 55+, $19.95 for ages 5-11
- For haunted encounters: $27.95, $24.95, and $15.95
- For general admission: $24.95, $21.95, and $12.95

Tours: Paranormal tours are:

- $50 for the Friday and Sunday tours starting at 8 p.m.
- $75 for the Friday tour that includes the use of ghost-hunting equipment and starts at midnight.
- $109 for the Saturday tour that includes dinner at the upscale Sir Winston's Restaurant and begins at 7 p.m.

Restaurants: All restaurants validate parking.

- Sir Winston's is open from 5:30 to 10 p.m. daily and is an upscale eatery with a dress code.
- Chelsea is open from 5:30 to 10 p.m. daily and is an upscale eatery without a strict dress code.
- Promenade Cafe is open from 6:00 a.m. to 10 p.m. daily and is a casual dining eatery.
- One of the best Sunday brunches can be found in the Grand Salon (formerly the 1st class dining hall) from 9:30 a.m. to 2 p.m.

Rancho Camulos...the "Home of Ramona."

Rancho Camulos

Rancho Camulos is a rarity in California in that it is probably the most famous place in the state that no one has ever heard of. This small, now insignificant farm on the far eastern outskirts of Ventura County was at one time the driving force behind a surge of immigration into this state and an important part of the agricultural base of the area.

Originally a Native American village named Kamulus and used in the early 1800s by the Mission San Fernando Rey de Espania for farming and grazing, it became part of a land grant — the 48,600-acre San Francisco Rancho — given to Antonio del Valle in 1839 for his service to the King and Queen of Spain.

Antonio was a native of Compostela, Mexico. He came to California in 1819 as a lieutenant in the infantry tasked with bringing troops to the Presidio in San Francisco. The fort had been having problems with raiders and more troops were needed to help protect its walls. Antonio del Valle became commander of Monterey in 1822 and served in that post up to 1834 when he was put in charge of the Mission San Fernando. He served in that position until 1837; two years later he received his land grant.

After Antonio's death in 1841, the property passed on to his son, Ygnacio, who began construction of his home on the site we now know as Rancho Camulos. The first structures to be erected were a four-room adobe house and a corral for the horses. After settlement of a land dispute involving his stepmother, Ygnacio bought up some of the remaining family property at the nearby Rancho Temescal to the north and began raising livestock. During construction and the early years of the rancho, and mostly due to the fact that Ygnacio was a state legislator, the del Valles lived in Los Angeles on Olvera Street and turned over the day-to-day operations of Camulos to Jose Antonio Salazar. Having inherited Camulos, buying Temescal, and having been granted Rancho Tejon in 1843 as a reward for his military service, Ygnacio became one of the largest landowners in the state.

Among the crops grown at Camulos was the first commercially-grown Valencia oranges in Ventura County, an extensive crop of wine grapes, and an almond grove. At first, the output of oranges was small and the crops had to be shipped to Los Angeles by cart along the El Camino Real, which, at best, was a narrow dirt road, but by 1876 the Southern Pacific Railroad traversed the town of Saugus, which was only seventeen miles distant and gave Camulos a nearby shipping site.

Ygnacio moved his family to Rancho Camulos in 1861 and over the intervening years the adobe was expanded to house his growing family and to entertain his many guests. A brick winery was built, along with a chapel and a workers' dorm. For a few years, the large estate prospered; however, a drought hit the area in the mid-1860s that forced Ygnacio to sell off much of his land. Thomas Scott sold the 1,500 acres of Rancho Camulos back to the Del Valle family. Ygnacio reduced that acreage even more by giving land to his oldest son, Juventino, who had taken over the duties of managing the ranch. Even with all the hardships and loss, Rancho Camulos not only survived, but also flourished. By 1870, seven more children were born and the ranch house grew to have twenty rooms, along with an extension to the north adding to one of the wings.

By the time Ygnacio died in 1880, the rancho had been reduced to 1,290 acres of land, but its crops had grown from a few hundred orange trees to having almonds, walnuts, avocados, vegetables, and a large vineyard. It had its own winery, chapel, cattle, and roughly two hundred residents employed and living on the ranch.

It was the wine grapes that helped sustain the rancho through the lean years. In the 1860s, ninety acres were planted and wine and brandy were produced shortly after. By 1870, forty-five tons were harvested and over 5,000 gallons of wine and 800 gallons of brandy were produced. The quality of the potables was so high that a reputation of excellence was attached to Camulos throughout the area.

Ygnacio's son, Juventino, served as manager of the estate from 1862 until 1886, when Ulpiano del Valle took over at the age of twenty-one after graduating from college. One of the first things Ulpiano did was to bring high-class horses to the ranch and began raising them for the racetrack. However, it was the year 1884, two years before Ulpiano would take over, that an event would change the rancho and the del Valle family forever.

The long back porch of the rancho!

Not much wine comes out of the Camulos' winery today!

The chapel at Rancho Camulos.

In 1882, a woman by the name of Helen Hunt Jackson visited the ranch. She only spent a few hours there, but in that short time her mind would pick up the minute details of everyday life and spawn a story that even today has a direct impact on Camulos and the surrounding area. Jackson's book *Ramona* was published in 1884 and the backdrop of the story is Rancho Camulos.

The story is that of Ramona, a Native American girl, and the trials and sorrows she goes through while employed at the "Moreno Ranch." On the East Coast, the book was a huge bestseller. The romance and splendor of California mission life, real or imagined, was now in the minds of people who dreamed of travel and adventure. In 1887, a photographer for the *San Francisco Chronicle* recreated scenes from *Ramona* using del Valle family members in the roles of the characters from the book. These pictures, and the numerous postcards being produced as "Ramona originals," along with the opening of the Southern Pacific station near Camulos, caused a veritable tidal wave of tourists to descend on the quiet family ranch.

The relatively secluded location and the lack of access to the rancho did not deter the tourists and Camulos was in no way set up to receive these guests. The del Valle family, however, with their Old World hospitality, would lodge and feed the multitudes arriving at their door. By the fall of 1888, it was becoming so expensive for the family that Reginaldo urged his mother Ysabel to stop being so accommodating and was even thinking about building a hotel on the property to house the visitors and to make it more profitable. The tourists themselves were beginning to become quite a problem, as they would steal items from the house, trample through the crops, and help themselves to fruit and vegetables right off the trees. This was all having an effect on Ysabel in her later years and worried the family to no end.

The del Valle family did capitalize on the fame of the book *Ramona* and the fact that it was widely believed to be Rancho Camulos that was the setting for the book. They branded their wine and oranges "Home of Ramona Brand" and used the same view of the veranda that was seen in many of the Ramona postcards. It is said that one of the native employees even portrayed herself as Ramona and made quite a bit of money charging for photographs.

It was this idea of California life portrayed in *Ramona* and the tales of tourists once they returned home that induced Americans in large numbers to pull up roots back East and in the Midwest and head to the Pacific Coast with expectations of grand adventure and exotic peoples.

By 1900, Ulpiano del Valle had expanded the ranch by increasing the orchards, planting new crops, and adding livestock. When the Southern Pacific Railroad relocated its line away from Rancho Camulos, the family assumed that the tourists would finally stop arriving at their gate, but that was not to be. Friction within the family and the death of key family members forced the sale of Camulos. In 1924, the rancho was sold to a Swiss immigrant by the name of August Rubel, who had been in the area for many years and owned the Billiwhack Dairy just down the road from Camulos.

It was in the latter part of June 1999 that my daughter was to be married. We had booked the chapel and grounds of Rancho Camulos for the event because of the sheer beauty of the place. My daughter thought it would be a perfect setting for her special day. The price was right also, but that was a mere formality in consideration for my baby's wedding day.

The day started off as I would assume most wedding days do, with everyone running around like headless chickens making sure the tables and chairs are set properly, the caterer has gotten everything right, the minister has arrived, and the groom has not gotten cold feet and run off to Mexico. The small chapel does not hold many people, but there is room outside the doors for people to sit on long benches, so we needed to make sure the speaker system was operating at the right volume and the flowers were all where they needed to be. Once everything was perfect, it was time to relax and wait for the moment I have dreaded all my adult life: giving my daughter away to someone else.

My daughter had been in seclusion inside the original adobe house getting ready with her bridesmaids who were also making sure that her soon-to-be husband did not sneak in to get an early view of his bride. I knocked on the door and her maid of honor answered and let me in. I asked how everything was going and my daughter said, "Great, one of the docents came in and gave us some tips on how to tie our dress bows to make them a bit fancier." She showed me the intricate bows they had tied and told me the docent had walked them through the tying. I asked who this docent was and they said her name was Isabel. It was getting late, so I told the girls they should take their places in the chapel and I was going to stay until it was time to walk Jess down the aisle. We talked quietly for ten minutes or so until we were called to the church. As we walked across the lawn to the chapel, my daughter pointed toward this large birdcage and said, "That's Isabel right there." I looked back as Jess waved and saw an older lady in Old Spanish dress look back at her with a smile and a nod. I waved at her also and she smiled at me as well.

The ceremony went well with tears all around, including myself, and the reception went off without a hitch. Jess, her mother, and I sat and talked with her new husband and she kept telling us how Isabel had such a calming effect on her — the way she talked and smiled while she got ready and how it was almost as if she had been a grandmother figure telling her how her life would be once she was married. I noticed that every time Jess mentioned Isabel a smile would come to her face, and I decided I needed to make sure Isabel was properly thanked for her support of my daughter.

After the reception was over and my daughter had departed on her honeymoon and the staff was busy cleaning up, I looked for Isabel to thank her. I found the staff member who had kept an eye on the place during our event and asked her if Isabel was still around or had she gone home already. The staff member looked confused and said they had no one by that name working or volunteering at Camulos. I explained what had transpired, which caused even more confusion for the poor woman. She had no idea who the lady could be and the only person she knows of by that name was the long-dead matriarch of the del Valle family. She pointed out a picture of Isabel del Valle and I was stunned to realize that it was the same woman I had seen in the garden earlier that day. I didn't mention this fact to the staff member I was talking to and I have never said anything to my daughter for fear that it might mar her otherwise happy day, but I will never be able to explain, even to myself, how it was possible for us to have this interaction with a woman who had been dead for many years.

~ Nathan Donaldson

August Rubel continued to run the farm as it was, employed many of the same ranch hands, and used the same labels as the del Valles. Some of the changes Rubel made at Camulos were to add more orange trees and he constructed a school for his five children. Some of his employees' children would also attend this small school, most notably those of his foreman and accountant. Chickens, cows, and turkeys were brought in and raised, along with a tropical bird aviary built for his wife. Rubel also installed the concrete paths we see today at the site. It was August Rubel who established the first museum at Camulos in the winery to store and show the del Valle family belongings to those "Ramona seekers" that still came to see the ranch. The new owners, however, made it clear that Camulos was a private residence and discouraged visitors from violating their privacy.

Rubel had served in the Army Signal Corps in 1917 and when World War II broke out he reenlisted. In 1943, while driving an ambulance in Tunisia, his vehicle hit a German mine and he was killed. His wife remarried in 1946 to Edwin Burger, and they lived and managed Camulos until 1968, when Rubel's widow passed away. After Mary's death, Burger shut the ranch down and it was left to decay for many years. After the Northridge earthquake in 1994, the Rubel family heirs gained control and began restoring the buildings to their former glory. In 1996, the Rubel family had Rancho Camulos listed on the National Register of Historic Places and in 2000 it was designated a National Historic Landmark.

Paranormal Activity

One of the better known paranormal stories at Rancho Camulos does not involve spirits per se, but that of a cryptozoological creature known as the Billiwhack Monster. There is some speculation as to the origins of this legend, as well as its validity. Locals have postulated that the monster was one of August Rubel's experiments gone awry. They say he was employed by the pre-CIA department Office of Strategic Services (OSS) during the intervening years between the wars and was tasked to create a "super soldier." Another version has it that a group of Nazi scientists were captured by the OSS and had a secret base built under the Billiwhack dairy, where the scientists were to create these same super soldiers. Either way, August Rubel figures prominently in the stories as an OSS operative. It is even mentioned that his death in Tunisia was the OSS making sure Rubel stayed quiet about the happenings at his dairy.

The story goes that the Nazi scientists or Rubel himself sabotaged their work and killed the creatures they had made except for one that managed to escape into the surrounding countryside. The Nazis were then executed and the story covered up. Whichever story one wants to put to this legend, one thing that all the stories have in common are the tales of the creature's looks and the way it acts. It is described as an ape-like humanoid with long claws, long, curving horns, stands eight feet tall, and has incredible strength. "He looks as if he is a cross between a man and a goat."

The first time anyone heard of this creature was in the 1950s, when a nine-year-old boy came home late and told his parents he had been attacked "by a strange creature." When the child arrived, his parents noticed he had scratches covering both arms and his back. The authorities were called, but no sign of the monster could be found. The sightings continued after that, but mostly by teenagers and children. The tales range from rocks as heavy as sixty pounds being thrown at cars to the creature approaching and smashing car hoods with a large club it is known to carry. In 1964, the Billiwhack Monster reportedly stalked several hikers for several hours, which prompted the group to contact the press. The subsequent story brought the legend out in the open and more news stories followed.

The *Los Angeles Times* did a story on the Billiwhack Monster sometime in the 1960s and included the tale of a boy being picked up by police because he was carrying a sword. It was the child's intent to confront and slay the beast. Another recounted a tale by a resident of how she had detained a large group of "Billiwhack hunting" children until police arrived to send them home. The reaction of the police to the fact that she had used a shotgun to keep the kids in line is not mentioned. I leave it to my intrepid readers to make up their own minds on the validity of these tales, but while at Rancho Camulos one should keep an open eye and a keen ear.

Other tales of the paranormal include guests that have been shoved in the main gathering room of the adobe, strange noises coming from the upstairs rooms when there is no one present, and voices calling out visitors' names at random times. Rob Wladarski, anthropologist, archeologist, author, and paranormal investigator, has performed a number of séances at Camulos and discovered that any mention of August Rubel is usually met with a heavy oppressive feeling permeating the area and is accompanied by an order to "not speak about Rubel!" In the room once occupied by Edwin Burger, Mary Rubel's second husband, the feeling of wanting to be alone is strong and it is known that Edwin was a very private person. It would seem he is asking to be left alone. The chapel has been known to give strange EVP activity, as well as all of the rooms in the adobe. Planet Paranormal was not fortunate enough to get any evidence that was noteworthy during their investigation of the Rancho; however, reviewing the evidence of others while there leads us to give Camulos a moderate in paranormal activity.

Today, Rancho Camulos is a quiet, out-of-the-way place used for weddings and gatherings in a unique and peaceful setting. It is hard to believe that this wonderful piece of California history was once a busy ranch and tourist destination. Walking its shaded paths, people don't realize that here was one of the major draws of immigration into the state of California or that a simple work of fiction would one day send thousands of people flocking to this corner of Ventura County.

There are several buildings open to the public as part of the Rancho Camulos Museum. All of the buildings are in their original locations and were built before 1930. The main house, known as the Yganacio del Valle adobe, is in the process of being completely restored and the landscaping is in pristine condition and includes a garden, ornamental trees, walkways, and fountain. To the west of the main house is the largest black walnut tree in the area and its branches span almost half an acre.

Rancho Camulos is indeed a beautiful place and well worth the effort to see. There is a small fruit stand at the entrance and a gift shop in the old school building. While you are there, shop, pick up a copy of *Ramona*, and, perhaps, donate badly needed money for restoration. Look around at the history and imagine what it must have been like in the early days of California. If you need help, ask the old residents your questions. It would appear that they are still here, giving their hospitality to visitors who are respectful by welcoming them into their home.

RANCHO CAMULOS

5164 E. Telegraph Road	Visitor Information
(Highway 126)	Museum hours: Saturdays, 1 to 4 p.m.
Piru, CA 93040	Tours: Hourly at 1, 2, and 3 p.m.;
805-521-1501	also by appointment

The Workman/Shadow Ranch today.

Shadow Ranch

The San Fernando Valley is well known nowadays for the dumb, self-centered valley girl of song and movie fame, but the Valley is also home to many historic adobe structures and ranchos, not the least of which is the old Workman Ranch. Today, it is known as Shadow Ranch and is a community center for the Los Angeles Parks Department. However, this house situated in a small park in this urban jungle has had a profound impact on the growth of the whole Los Angeles area.

Around 1850, Isaac Van Nuys created the San Fernando Valley Homestead Association and began planting dry wheat on rich farmland in the west valley. Under Van Nuys's leadership, the ranch grew to contain 9,000 acres and was incorporated as the Los Angeles Farm and Milling Company. During this growth period, an Australian immigrant by the name of Albert Workman was hired as foreman and superintendent.

By 1869, Workman had saved enough money to buy the ranch outright and purchased an additional 4,000 acres to cultivate. Over time, Workman added seventy barns, 1,000 head of cattle, numerous wagons to transport the wheat to Los Angeles, and built a two-story ranch house for his family. The house would become the centerpiece of the property and was built to accommodate not only Workman's family, but it could also easily seat over sixty workers for meals in the forty-foot-long room that spanned the entire west side of the home.

The Workman Ranch was not only known for its wheat crop, but it's also famous as the spot where the first eucalyptus trees were planted in all of Southern California. Albert, being homesick for his native Australia, imported Blue Gum eucalyptus seeds and planted them around his ranch in the 1870s and these trees would become the parent plants of all the others in Southern California — or so the legend goes. These trees grew to great heights and, with its foliage, provided shade all over the ranch property.

Unfortunately, the Valley began to grow in popularity and land became a priority for the many people flocking to the area. The ranch land acres slowly dwindled and, as the crops diminished, so did the wealth of the family; the structures began to deteriorate, including the family home, and by 1930 was in need of restoration. It was at this time that the property was sold to Florence Ryerson and Colin Clements. The two were both successful screenwriters for the Hollywood film studios and were able to fully restore the ranch house to its former glory. In honor of the many eucalyptus trees providing an enormous amount of cooling shade in the otherwise scorching Valley heat, the two decided to rename the property Shadow Ranch. Florence Ryerson wrote one of the world's most beloved screenplays, *The Wizard of Oz*, while living at the ranch.

The property was again sold in 1950, and the house was transformed into a private school called "Robinayre School for Girls" and the old carriage house was converted into a dormitory called "The Little House." The school only lasted for a few years and the property became vacant. In 1961, it was used in the filming of a screen adaptation of a Lillian Hellman play; the film, *The Children's Hour*, was directed by William Wyler, who had seen the ranch while driving past one day and thought it would be the perfect setting for his film.

Afraid that the ranch would become just another eyesore and demolished to make way for more urban housing, the Los Angeles City Council declared the residence as Cultural-Historic Monument #9 on November 2, 1962, thereby saving the historic abode for future generations. Today, Shadow Ranch sits on thirteen acres, all that is left of the original 13,000, and is owned by the Los Angeles City Parks and Recreation Department, which uses the old house as a community center. The rest of the property is being utilized as a city park, with the eucalyptus trees still providing shade, now for families on picnics and children at play on those long, hot summer days in the Valley.

Paranormal Activity

No one knows why people linger after death as ghosts and just as confusing is why they would pick certain areas to dwell in the afterlife. Shadow Ranch has never had a violent death associated with it (that can be confirmed) and everything history tells us is that the ranch was a peaceful place to not only live, but to work as well.

The Shadow Ranch carriage house.

The "hidden" room in the closet at Shadow Ranch.

This being said, it is clear that past residents and guests have decided that Shadow Ranch is the place to spend their eternity.

As early as the 1950s, paranormal activity has been reported at the old ranch house. During its incarnation as a girl's school, one of the cooks believed that a ghost was wandering around the yard and the garage area. This ghost, according to the cook, would on occasion also be seen walking a small hallway right next to the kitchen. Who this spirit might be is unknown, as the cook said he could never get a clear enough view to tell if it was male or female.

Since the ranch house has become a community center, the staff has reported a little girl who seems to appear almost every night at closing time. It seems that the girl is anxious that everyone leave so she can be alone in the house (at least with no living human) so she can have the upstairs playroom to herself. If the staff tends to linger, this little girl has been known to tug on a sleeve or arm…as if telling the employees that it is time to leave. This little girl is also sometimes seen throughout the day following staff or other children, as if curious about what they may be doing. It could be that she wants to play with the other children, but cannot seem to figure out how. She is wearing a blue dress and may have been a student of the Robinayre School, but her identity still remains a mystery.

Another of the ghosts that have been reported in the house is that of a little boy. People most often see him from the outside of the building peering down at them from one of the upstairs windows. Legend has it that this child was killed in a tragic accident that left him beheaded; unfortunately, no record of his death has ever emerged, so confirming this account is impossible. On very rare occasions, staff have seen this child ducking down hallways and through doors in an attempt to keep hidden.

Planet Paranormal has had the opportunity to investigate this location on two separate evenings with renowned paranormalist and author Rob Wlodarski. On both occasions, the little girl has made her presence known, along with other spirits who seem to occupy the residence. On one visit, while Rob was recording with an old style magnetic tape recorder, a spirit saying she was Florence Ryerson answered many questions. This was accomplished by asking a question with the tape recorder running and then playing the tape back to hear any answer that was given. The group gained some inside knowledge of Hollywood filmdom during this session. Unfortunately, these same recordings did not show up on any voice recorder, so the only record of this conversation is on "old school" (i.e. hard to transfer) equipment. Planet Paranormal rates this location as having mild to medium paranormal activity.

Today, the sound of children at play and the laughter of families replace the drone of farm equipment and the aroma of barbecue replaces the scent of the wheat. Events sponsored by the Parks and Recreation Department include movies at Halloween and youth group meetings in the old ranch house, but one thing is certain: the spirits of those who once called this place home are still watching over the property and seem to be pleased by what they see. However, one must remember that when the center closes for the night…that's when the other children come out to play and the spirits walk their old "haunt."

My friend was working with the Parks Department at the Shadow Ranch Children's Center and had been scheduled to work the shift that required her to stay and close up late. She always hated working this shift because it meant that the doors stayed open until 8 p.m. and she wouldn't get home until 10 or so. She had asked me if I could come by around 5 and hang out with her till close, but I told her that I had my son that night and wanted to spend time with him. She told me to bring him along and that he would love to play upstairs in the big play room. I figured that would be cool, so I told her "okay."

My son Darrell and I arrived at the Community Center a little after 6 and my friend got Darrell organized up in the playroom, and then she and I want back downstairs to the office so we could keep an eye on anyone entering the center. We hadn't been down in the office for long when I heard Darrell start to laugh. I thought this was a little weird since he was supposed to be alone with the toys upstairs. I decided to go have a look and see if someone had snuck into the center and was messing with my child. The door to the room is right at the top of the stairs and when I was about halfway up I realized that he was talking to someone. I stood on the top step for a few minutes and listened to my son carry on a conversation about the cars that he was playing with and it was clear that he heard somebody answering because it sounded to me like he was answering questions. I couldn't hear anyone, though. I had enough and opened the door, expecting to see another person in the room with Darrell. When I went in, though, there was nobody with him…he was alone.

I was a bit stunned that my son was alone in the playroom as I had just heard, or thought I had heard, him talking to someone. I asked him who it was and he pointed to the closet and said, "It was my friend." I went to the closet, but there was nobody there. I asked Darrell again who he had been talking to and told him he better not lie to me. Again, he just said, "My friend in the closet." I called down to my friend who came up and pointed out another, smaller door in the back of the closet. We went inside this little hidden room, but there was no one there, either. As my friend and I were coming out of this other room, we both heard Darrell start to giggle and we both thought we heard another voice laughing as well. We hurried out to where my son was, but again he was alone.

My friend and I split up and spent the next half-hour searching the center, but found nothing. I returned to my son and again tried to get him to tell me who his "friend" was and where he was hiding. Darrell just kept saying that he was in the closet and that he lived there. I told my son that I didn't like him lying to me and that we were leaving because of it. My friend was not happy about it, but understood.

A few days later, my friend called me and told me that she had talked to a coworker about what happened and that her coworker told her that the place was supposed to be haunted. I didn't believe her until I started to check it out for myself online. Sure enough, I found a few things about there being child ghosts at Shadow Ranch. I told Darrell I was sorry about calling him a liar.

~ Monisha Jameson

SHADOW RANCH

22633 Vanowan Street
West Hills, CA 91307
818-883-3637
shadowranch.recreationcenter@lacity.org

69

The *Star of India* regal with sails unfurled.

Star of India

Starting out life as the *Euterpe* in November 1863, the *Star of India* was a full-rigged, three-masted, iron sailing ship known as a windjammer. She had a varied career as a spice hauler, passenger ship, freight transport, lumber vessel, and now as a museum piece in San Diego Bay. She is the oldest vessel still sailing regularly and the oldest iron-hulled merchant ship still afloat. She is also said to be very haunted.

The *Euterpe's* first two voyages were fraught with trouble. On her maiden voyage in January 1864, under the command of Capt. William Storry, she was dispatched to Calcutta to transport a load of spice back to England. Leaving Liverpool in the evening, she was sailing off the coast of Wales when she was hit by an unlit Spanish brig. The damage to the ship was such that the crew refused to continue with the cruise and the captain was forced to return to port for repairs; seventeen crewmembers were sentenced to hard labor for their failure to obey the commands of their commander. Her second sailing in 1865 would start out much better, but would see more damage to the ship and the death of her captain. While sailing in the Bay of Bengal, a squall appeared and quickly grew to become a gale. The wind was so severe that two of the masts had to be cut away and the ship limped into Calcutta, where she would have a prolonged stay to make repairs. On the return trip to England, Captain Storry became ill and died; he was buried at sea.

These two unfortunate voyages caused the owners to believe that the ship was "unlucky" and they decided to sell her. The *Euterpe* was sold to David Brown of London and the ship made four uneventful crossings to India and back; however, with the rise of steamships and the opening of the Suez Canal, Mr. Brown found that a sailing ship was just not cost effective, and in 1871, the ship was again sold, this time to Shaw, Savill & Company. The ship was used to ferry New Zealand immigrants and freight to England. These voyages, however, were always eastbound and took hundreds of days to complete. The *Euterpe* would make ports of call in Australia, California, Chile, and stops in the Caribbean before heading across the Atlantic to the British Isles. The *Euterpe* would continue in this capacity for the next twenty-five years.

In 1897, the ship was sold to a Hawaiian company, and was used to ferry supplies between the islands. This lasted until 1899 when the *Euterpe* was sold to the Pacific Colonial Ship Company of San Francisco. In this stage of her life, the sailing vessel made voyages between the Pacific Northwest, Hawaii, and Australia, carrying sugar, coal, and lumber. These owners held onto her for two years, selling her again in 1901.

Sold to the Alaska Packers Association, the ship underwent a complete rigging change in San Francisco. Having her rear mast removed, she became a two-masted barque and began transporting fishermen, coal, and supplies to the Bering Sea and returning with a hold full of salmon and other cold water fish. The company registered her in the United States and in 1902 changed her name to the *Star of India.*

Steam power was on the rise and the company had to change with the times or go out of business, so in 1923, after twenty-two Alaskan voyages, the ship was put in dock as a relic of the old ways. For three years, the grand ship sat rusting at the wharf and then, in 1926, she was sold to the San Diego Zoological Society to become the centerpiece of their planned aquarium and museum. However, this had to be shelved when the Great Depression hit, followed by the world being plunged into war. For years, the ship sat…forgotten and decaying.

As luck would have it, in 1957, while on a speaking tour, an author and former windjammer captain happened to see the *Star of India* rusting in the harbor. His love of sailing could not allow him to stay silent and he began to publicize the plight of the ship. In 1959, a group of citizens from San Diego read his articles and formed the "Star of India Auxiliary," with the hope of raising enough money and awareness to save the old windjammer from the scrap heap. Slowly, money and support trickled in. Bit by bit and brush stroke by brush stroke, the regal ship gradually began to look like her old self. It would not be until 1976 that the *Star of India* would again take to the water. With great fanfare, she was put out to sea for trials and passed with flying colors.

Today, the *Star of India* is the pride of the San Diego Maritime Museum and is kept completely seaworthy. She is sailed at least once a year, hosts docent-led tours, and provides a "total immersion" overnight sleep aboard program for schools and youth groups. There are three other such ships afloat in the United States: the *USS Constitution*, the *Charles W. Morgan*, and *the USS Constellation*; however, none of these ships are seaworthy. Also, unlike these other three sailing vessels, the *Star of India* is almost 100% original from her hull to her cabins. The ship is sailed entirely by volunteers, usually within sight of land, around San Diego County. Her voyages are often not more than a day, but on rare occasions she is out of port longer.

A meet-up group I belong to had scheduled a private investigation of the *Star of India* in San Diego so I jumped at the chance to participate. I have been an amateur ghost hunter for thirty years and had always wanted to check out this boat. I live in Arizona, so it was a bit of a drive, but it was one of those trips that was well worth it.

We all met up on Friday night at 11 p.m. and were given the rules regarding our behavior while onboard. We were given a short informative tour and then were free to go investigate on our own. We broke up into three groups: one group took the lowest deck, one the middle, and one the upper; we would rotate after an hour with the upper group going to the middle deck, etc., and then after three hours we would all gather on the upper deck to go over any events that may have occurred. I was in the group that started on the middle deck, but it was kind of hard to investigate with a group above and one below making noise, so we just sort of found a section that was quiet and tried to do an EVP session. A couple of us wandered around snapping pictures and hoping for some evidence. After an hour, we rotated to the lowest deck, where we had to contend with what I was told was shrimp chattering like crazy on the hull of the boat. This made doing any audio impossible, but I did have fun on the little trolley that moves along the bottom of the boat through that tube going to the bow.

An hour later, we were on the upper deck and actually able to conduct a proper investigation. Once we were in the officers' quarters, we sat down at the table that takes up the middle of the room and set up for an audio session. We had barely gotten started when we heard a low moan coming from one of the rooms on the starboard side of the boat. It sounded like someone was in pain; we knew that everyone from our group was sitting at the table, but figured maybe an investigator from the other group stayed behind, possibly with a case of seasickness. "Jim" said he would check it out and went to look for whoever it was. He came back a short time later and said he couldn't find anyone. "Jim" sat back down and we again started asking questions of the spirits and once again we began to hear the moaning. This time "Jim" looked at the rooms on the port side while I got up and stood listening on the starboard. Sure enough, I heard the moan again and knew which room it had come from. I moved closer to the room, heard the sound once more, and then entered the small cabin. There was no one there and it was too small a room to hide anyone.

The rest of the group at this point had gotten up from their seats and came over to where I was standing in the little room. I told them I was sure that the sound had come from here and a couple others said the same thing. There had been five recorders going at the time we heard the moans, so we played back each one. Sure enough, you could just make out the sound on all five, but it gave no indication of where it might have originated. We all headed back to the table a bit confused, but all pretty sure we had caught something paranormal. "Shirley" had been the last one out of the room and had noticed the small plaque next to the room telling people whose room it was. As it turns out, the cabin that we kept hearing the moan coming from was that of the ship's doctor. Could it be that what we had all heard was the pain of a sailor who had been injured long ago and died in the doctor's care? Was he still here in pain? We may never know, but at least we have evidence that someone is still there.

Like I said before, it may have been a long drive from Phoenix, but after the night I had investigating the *Star of India*, it was definitely worth the trip. I will go again if I ever have the opportunity. I just hope that if there is a wounded sailor still there that we may be able to help him pass on some day and find some peace.

~ Mitch Cullen

Paranormal Activity

The *Star of India*, although unable to keep any one owner for more than a year or two, still had a rich and vibrant sailing career. Maybe it's because she couldn't keep an owner that the ship is so haunted. Many tales of footsteps, unexplained odors, sounds, and orbs have been reported for years even before she was cast as a museum and relic.

The galley is one of these areas. Visitors report that they can smell the aroma of bread cooking and sometimes stew or soup. They have asked the docents if the food is being prepared for an overnight stay and are baffled when they find that the ship's stoves no longer function and have been cold for decades. Other times the pots and pans are seen moving...even though the water is calm and the ship is still.

At the start of one of her voyages, as the crew was hoisting the anchor chain, they were unaware that one of their crew mates had gone into the chain locker. The Chinese crewman did not realize that the order to get underway had been given and was trapped in the compartment, and he was slowly crushed to death as the heavy chain fell upon him. Though he screamed loudly and for as long as he could, the others could not hear him over the roar of the hoisting machinery. His body lay under the cold metal until the anchor was again lowered. Today, there are reports of cold spots around the opening of the chain locker and visitors sometimes claim to hear what they believe to be a man screaming for help. The voice, however, seems to come from far away.

In the crew's quarters, people have reported cold spots and many get a strange and sharp feeling of fear. No one knows why this emotion is so prevalent here, but the theory is that if a crewman suffered an injury he would be brought to his bunk. Many ships in those days did not have proper medical capabilities, so the sailors with serious conditions may have known they were going to die and the ship may have absorbed their feelings of terror.

The most well-known haunt of the *Star of India* is that of a young stowaway by the name of John Campbell. John was a child really and when he was found he was put to work rather than put overboard. In 1884, stowaways were still treated very harshly, but it is believed that the young man's age played a part in the Captain's leniency. It was decided that the young lad would work off his passage as a deckhand. The other crewmen taught him the ways of the sea — knots, rigging, sail-mending, and storm preparation — and he seemed to take to the tasks and got along well with the others.

One day, when young John was sent high up in the rigging, he lost his footing in the ropes and fell one hundred feet to the deck. He survived, but was hurt badly. He was taken below deck, where he laid in agony for three days until he passed away. The crew buried him at sea the following day. Today, visitors hear his footfalls and sometimes report feeling a small, cold hand grasp theirs when they are near the area of the ship where Campbell fell to the deck. Some have even reported getting his image on camera.

The *Star of India* was made for the wind.

One of the *Star of India*'s permanent passengers and a creepy one for investigators.

Planet Paranormal did not capture any activity or EVP while investigating this wonderful ship and it is for this reason that we rate the *Star of India* at mild to moderate paranormal activity.

The San Diego Maritime Museum has a number of ships in its collection; the *Star of India* is the only one still seaworthy, though the others are still a must-see for anyone with a love of the ocean and its great old ships. The *USS Midway* aircraft carrier is docked a short distance away and offers tours also. The *Star of India* is one of the best examples of an old sailing vessel afloat today and should not be missed if you happen to be in the San Diego area. She sits at the wharf and one has but to look at her to see how this grand lady still yearns for the waves under her keel. If you are lucky to be able to watch her depart on one of her short voyages around the San Diego area, look closely and you may be able to see those men who still crew her from a long-ago era and see how they care for this maiden of the sea. While touring her decks, keep alert for the sounds and smells of life as it was and say hello to those long-dead crewmen who still welcome you aboard.

STAR OF INDIA

1306 Harbor Drive
San Diego, CA 92106
619-234-9153

Thee Anaheim White House.
Photo courtesy of Rob Wlodarski.

Congratulations Bruno
A CNN Top 20
Hero of the World

Thee Anaheim White House Restaurant

When we hear the term "White House," we immediately think of the palatial temporary home of our elected head of state in Washington, D.C., but here in California we have Thee White House, which anyone can go to for dinner without the inherent pat down and background check involved with an invitation to the People's House. I am, of course, referring to the award-winning restaurant formerly known as Thee White House Restaurant in Anaheim, California. If you are wondering why "the" is spelled a bit differently, it is because the phrase "The White House" cannot be copyrighted, hence "Thee." The establishment is now known as The Anaheim White House Restaurant.

Built circa 1909 by Dosithe Gervais, it represents the classic Colonial Revival architecture that was popular at that time. Born in 1872 in Illinois, Gervais made his way to Los Angeles at the age of twenty-one and took employment with the Southern Pacific Railroad as a telegraph operator and freight manager. Having a wife, Alberta, and two daughters, Gladys and Violet, Dosithe began looking for a place with more room and a job that would allow him to spend more time with his family. He found what he was looking for in the remote farming community of Anaheim. Mr. and Mrs. Gervais purchased 2.5 acres of good growing land on almost barren South Los Angeles Street and began building their dream home. It is believed that they may have lived in a smaller structure on the land while the house was being built, but there are some conflicting reports on this.

While the construction was in progress, Gervais was busy planting strawberries and Valencia orange trees on seven acres surrounding the site. His first crop sold for $2,000, which convinced him that the citrus industry was going to be an important commodity. At this time, Gervais also began a nursery on the side and became a pioneer who experimented with varieties of oranges and sold only those that, in his opinion, were the cream of the crop. It was through his efforts, along with many others, that helped put Orange County in the public view. In total, Gervais had about 15,000 trees directly on his property and an additional 35,000 on surrounding land that he leased.

When the 3,842-square-foot, $5,000 dollar home was complete, it was a showpiece from the beginning. French doors, along with porch areas in the front and south side, lent an elegant and welcoming area for guests and wide, airy windows created a bright and pleasant place to live. By the time the house was ready to be occupied, the Gervais family had grown by one, with the birth of their third daughter, Dorothy. As teenage daughters are wont to do, they held many parties at the residence; however, due to Mr. Gervais's position in the community as an elected trustee of the school board, alcohol was strictly forbidden at these parties.

The Gervais family lived in the house until 1916, when they sold the property to George Waterman and his wife. The Watermans, however, would only live in the house for a short while; they sold the residence in 1919 to the family who would give its name to the home and to the man whom the people of Anaheim will always remember, Dr. John Truxaw and family.

John Truxaw was a graduate of University of Southern California Medical School and moved to Anaheim in 1912 to open a small private practice. Knowing that the community was in its infancy and that many of the patients he would be treating were, if not poor, of modest means, Dr. Truxaw refused to turn away anyone in need of his help. He was often seen after hours miles away from home in the far reaches of the canyons and hills making house calls. His weekends were spent treating his patients and he very rarely took vacations.

Dr. Truxaw and his wife, Louise, had eight children; their five boys used the top floor for their living quarters while the girls and the elder Truxaws used the other rooms in the house as theirs. Having that many children, parties of all sorts were constantly being held at the residence for birthdays, first communions, and many other childhood events. The home became a place of happiness, not only for the Truxaw children, but for their friends as well.

As if Dr. Truxaw was not busy enough, he also took on the responsibility of becoming the city's lone City Health Officer. Because of these duties, along with his devotion to making house calls on his many patients, his white car became a fixture in the City of Anaheim. As the health official, some of his many duties included examining the drunks brought in by the police, doing health inspections, and closing or condemning those places that failed, as well as keeping an eye out for contagious diseases and setting up quarantines and warning signs if any were found. It was because of this latter responsibility that he might have caused the burning of Chinatown and the dislocation of many of its inhabitants.

Stairway to the upper floor.

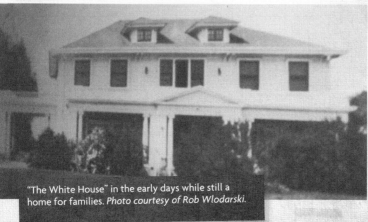

"The White House" in the early days while still a home for families. *Photo courtesy of Rob Wlodarski.*

Truxaw was also a charter member of St. Joseph Hospital and helped grow it into one of the largest hospitals in Orange County. He would volunteer his services to the patients when time allowed and sometimes when it didn't. The rest of the family was also involved with various charity works through the organizations of St. Boniface Catholic Church.

Dr. John Truxaw passed away in 1952 at the age of eighty-nine. It is estimated that in his forty years of practice the good doctor delivered over 3,500 babies spanning three generations, some of which were children born to children he delivered years earlier. His wife, Louise, would live in the home until her death in 1969 and together they would raise their family to include many grandchildren and great-grandchildren who are still active in the community today. It is due to the dedication and love of the town by Dr. John that the house will forever be known as The Truxaw House on the National Registry of Historic Places.

After Louise Truxaw passed, the house sat in limbo while the estate was being settled and became a rental. Most of the tenants treated the old home as they would their own, but in 1977, the house was turned into an alcohol rehabilitation center and the residents were anything but respectful of the property. The walls had holes punched into them, the cupboard doors were all removed and used as firewood on cold nights, and when the management company inspected the home after the "recovered" alcoholics moved out, they found the house littered with trash and empty wine bottles. The entire interior of the residence was severely neglected and needed extensive — and expensive — repair.

In 1978, an elderly woman in her 70s was looking to establish a business to help offset her retirement. Mrs. Bouck was never fond of being idle and saw the Truxaw home as a project that would be perfect for her vision of opening an upscale antique store. She repaired the cupboards and walls, upgraded the kitchen, and installed new carpet and fresh paint throughout. Mrs. Bouck had expected to spend an additional $60,000 to refurbish the home, but after all was said and done she had spent just over $100,000 to bring the grand old building back up to code. Unfortunately, due to failing eyesight and health problems, she was never able to see her dream come to fruition and she was unable to open her shop.

Owning several large motels around the Disneyland area, James Stovall would drive past the old home on a daily basis. He would think to himself how the land would be perfect for a condominium complex. When he found out that Mrs. Bouck had again put the property on the market, he jumped at the chance to purchase the residence. After the sale went through, Stovall immediately hired architect J. Ward Dawson to design the buildings for his new project. James' wife, Barbara (Bobbie), fell in love with the house from the moment she first saw it, but did not say anything to her husband regarding her disappointment about the forthcoming demolition. Bobbie was showing one of their friends the house when the woman told her that with the home's resemblance to the White House it would make a wonderful themed restaurant. Barbara loved the idea and mentioned it to James, along with her love of the house, and he agreed to consider the project. On the eve of the home's destruction, Stovall told his wife that he loved the idea and Thee White House Restaurant was born.

New plans were drawn up and the work to transform the old house began in earnest. James Stovall completed most of the work on the interior with Bobbie as his chief decorator. He took great care to protect the original wood throughout the home, as well as the craftsman trim, doorjambs, and mantle pieces. Some of the walls needed to be removed and rooms reconfigured to make the interior into a dining establishment, but all care was taken to retain the feel of the old home. Exterior redone and landscaping complete, the new restaurant opened on January 15, 1982.

Always the showman, Stovall added a sense of the whimsical to the menu by playing on the restaurant's namesake. Some of the features were: The Preamble (appetizers), House Ways and Greens (salads), United Steaks, Border Relations (Mexican entrees), and the Magna Carta (Desserts). At first, Thee White House did well because of the combination of uniqueness and the desire of area residents to see the inside of the "haunted house," as some of the locals had started calling it. However, the food was of mediocre quality and after the novelty wore off, the business began to struggle. Stovall fired his partner, who had been in charge of all the food, and hired Carol Hammond-Ehrler to run the restaurant. With Ehrler at the helm, the old Truxaw home had become a gastric success and a fixture on the Anaheim landscape.

If Carol Hammond-Ehrler put Thee White House on the local and California maps, then the current owner, Bruno Serato, went one better and placed the restaurant on the national and world maps. A classically-trained chef who was born in Italy, Serato bought the property in 1987, upgraded the menu to Northern Italian, changed the name to The Anaheim White House Restaurant, and never looked back. Today, his clientele consist of not only the locals and tourists, but also a cornucopia of who's who. Some of the notables to dine at Mr. Serato's second home are fight promoter Don King, Ted Williams, Rodger Clemens, Pele and Franco Harris, and movie stars George Burns, Annette Funicello, Connie Francis, and Keenan Ivory Wayans. Naomi Judd, Jenny Craig, and Siegfried & Roy have also been spotted dining on Serato's wonderful food creations, as well as heads of state, such as the Crown Prince of Belgium, a Saudi Arabian princess, and even former president Jimmy Carter. Serato has even catered for Madonna on occasion.

Even with all of the celebrities who stop in, Serato is quick to say that it is his loyal customers and friends that are the most important to him. Many regulars are now treated as family and everyone who comes to enjoy a meal with Bruno is treated with the utmost courtesy in the hopes that the staff is serving not new customers, but new friends.

Bruno Serato does not stop with his patrons, however, as he is often found serving hundreds of meals to poor and under-served families and children, bringing a bit of joy to lives that desperately need some cheer. Serato has won a Medal of Freedom for his efforts, but that is nothing compared to the smiles on the faces of the people he helps.

I was with a local paranormal investigation team. We arrived at [Thee Anaheim White House Restaurant] about 9 p.m. and had a bite to eat. Later, as soon as the last customers had left the establishment, we set up for the night's investigation. This restaurant has several banquet rooms and a structure, which is separate from the main house, used for wedding receptions; two stories with a large yard and patio area. The establishment itself, with a long driveway and parking lots, take up the entire corner of the two streets that intersect it, except for a charbroiled hamburger place next door.

My first set up was a long banquet room upstairs where it has been reported a fellow has been seen in the north end of this room sitting in the corner. My stationary camera was focused on this corner and I left a digital recorder in the room as well. The team I was with was exploring the house and deciding where they wanted to do their EVP session. Two EVPs I caught in the long banquet hall were of a woman calling for a fellow named Matt, of which no such person was amongst our group that night, and what sounded like a child's voice, which gave a small murmur and sigh. Eventually, the team and I congregated together in a small room upstairs in the southwest corner of the house. At the time I believe the room was called "Bobby's"; the name has been changed since then. We had been told the spirit of a young girl had been heard in this room and the intent was to try and make contact with her. The room is about the size of a small bedroom and has a door with a glass window that leads to a hallway. From this window, you can look down the hallway and see the doorway to another, smaller banquet room.

As we progressed with the EVP session, I was standing with my camera, video recording the session, when I looked down the hallway towards the other room. The door to the other room was open and protruded out into the hallway at a 90° angle from the room itself. The door wagged liked the tail on a dog. I couldn't believe what I had just seen. It moved, side-to-side, back-and-forth, from left to right at least twice and then stopped, perfectly still, straight out from the room as it had been. Immediately, I told the team what I had just seen and they all scrambled down the hall to take a look at the door. A couple tested the door to see if it would move easily and they found that the rug on the floor was pretty snug up to the bottom of the door, which would mean it would take some force to move it. One or two of them jumped up and down by the door to see if the vibration would make it move; it did not. This door was not moving on its own. Also, being upstairs in the middle of the house, there was no crosscurrent or breeze that would move the door.

After some discussion, the team, except for one fellow, Brian, went back into "Bobby's" room to continue with the EVP session. I decided to set up my camera in the hall focused on the door. Bob, who was the team leader, went back into the long banquet room where our equipment was stored. Brian had ventured into the room where the moving door was to look around and perhaps do some EVP work. As I was finishing the set up of my camera, as if something was standing beside me, in my right ear something or someone gave a large grunt. Just as I heard this grunt, Brian was walking out of the room down the hall and at first I thought he had made the grunt. Bob heard the grunt all the way back in the room he was at. I was shocked and surprised; perhaps I wanted to believe it was Brian who grunted, but in reviewing the video, it was very clear it was not Brian. Just as Brian is coming out of the room down the hall, he is calling Bob's name and this is when the grunt occurs. Also in the video, just before the grunt, a small ball of light can be seen jetting from the end of the hallway towards me and that's when the grunt occurs. The grunt was loud enough to be heard throughout the house — there was nothing meek or dainty about it. Clearly, in my opinion, whatever made the grunt was male.

This was not the end of our adventure in the house this night, as Brian and I would have an interesting experience with a fellow who wanted some bourbon…but this is for another story. This house is real, and in my opinion the haunting that occurs there is real. Never take a place for granted.

~ Gerald Reynolds

Paranormal Activity

Over the years, as the Truxaw house sat idle and empty, its exterior fading in the harsh sun, wind, and the elements of nature, a tale sprang up that the house was haunted. Of course, every unoccupied home, if neglected long enough, will gain this reputation — as if the sheer fact of abandonment is an open house sign for spirits. This tale, however, just may have a shred of truth attached to it.

The most common spirit reported at Thee Anaheim White House Restaurant is that of a little girl. She is often seen on the front porch playing a game or singing. It is said that the child is the daughter of the home's builder, Dosithe Gervais; she was supposedly struck by a car or trolley while playing near the street and died before the doctor could arrive. This theory has never been substantiated and, in fact, has never had a shred of evidence ever linked to it. My theory is that Dr. Truxaw, who never turned away a patient, may have had a child brought to him who was injured or sick and was unable to prevent the girl's death. We may never know, but hopefully further investigation of the restaurant will garner more information.

There are other spirits residing at Thee Anaheim White House Restaurant that the staff have come to think of as family. Many of the staff have seen doors open or close on their own accord, have heard the sound of disembodied footsteps walking down the hallways, doorknobs turning on their own as one of the staff reach for them, and items moving from assigned areas that no living hand has touched. While dining at the restaurant, many customers have reported feeling as if energy has passed through them...almost as if a low-voltage electrical wire has touched them. Others have reported cold spots that are there one second and gone the next.

The upstairs rooms seem to have more activity than the lower floors and it is here that the lights will flicker, dim, and even go out at inopportune moments and then snap back on, leaving both guests and staff to wonder. People have even reported the feeling of someone or something passing through them, leaving them momentarily paralyzed and shivering. In the bar area of the restaurant, it is reported that a woman had her derriere pinched hard enough to leave a bruise.

Owner Bruno Serato has had his own encounter with the unknown. One night, while he was locking up, he had just turned on the alarms when he heard footsteps coming from the upstairs areas. To Serato, it sounded as if a child were running or playing and he was afraid that whomever was there was going to trip the alarms. As he went up the flight, he noticed a bluish light coming from the Blue Room. Going into the room, there was no one present and the light had vanished. A search of the building revealed no stowaway, and to this day Mr. Serato still cannot find a cause for the strange blue light.

During Planet Paranormal's investigation of Thee Anaheim White House Restaurant, we captured only a couple EVPs, but also caught on video, by friend and fellow investigator Gerald Reynolds, was a door moving on its own while at the same time a disembodied grunt could be heard. Other strange noises could be heard throughout the evening, but we could classify none as being paranormal in nature. The video is enough for us to classify this wonderful restaurant as having a medium to high paranormal rating.

There are many reasons that a home becomes haunted. Sometimes it's due to a tragic occurrence and other times it's because the spirit feels welcome and at home, but never just because it's abandoned. The Truxaw home, I am sure, is one of those places that invite warm feelings of peace and warmth. Now, with Mr. Serato's exquisite food choices and caring attitude for those less fortunate than himself, those feelings of home are magnified — not only for his dining family of friends, but also for those who remain from times past. No one who comes to Thee Anaheim White House Restaurant nor those who work there feel threatened in the least by the spirits that roam the old home's walls. On the contrary, as Mr. Serato has said, "I'm sure the spirits love what I've done with the place."

If you find yourself in the city of Anaheim and want to treat yourself to a first-rate, world-class dining experience, then a visit to Thee Anaheim White House Restaurant is a must. Good food, great wine, and wonderful company await and, if you happen to see Mr. Serato, tell him that Planet Paranormal sends their regards. Remember, though: the spirits at the bar are not the only spirits you will encounter, so if you see a little girl or her mother and they look a bit out of place, take a closer peek…you just may have seen the Truxaw family.

THEE ANAHEIM WHITE HOUSE RESTAURANT

887 S. Anaheim Boulevard
Anaheim, CA 92805
714-772-1381
www.anaheimwhitehouse.com

Vallecito Station, an oasis in the desert.

Vallecito Stage Station

The first Europeans arrived at the springs of Vallecito in 1782 when a troop of Spanish soldiers, led by Army Commandant Pedro Fages, was on its way back to San Diego from the Colorado River. They came across a village inhabited by the Hawi and dubbed the oasis Vallecito, Spanish for "Little Valley." They had originally wanted to build a Presidio, but lacked the population to keep it manned. The word was out, however, and it became a stopover for settlers, traders, and colonists on their way to the more populated areas of California. The first American troops to camp at Vallecito were a small group of men from the Army of the West, under the command of Stephen Watts Kearny in 1846 on its way to battle in the Mexican-American War. The Mormon Battalion followed later with the first wagons brought to the area.

When gold was discovered at Sutter's Mill in Northern California in 1849, prospectors and immigrants flocked to the gold fields in droves. Many of them used the southern route from Texas and then after crossing the Imperial Valley in what came to be known as "the journey of death" these travelers would stop at Vallecito to rest, tend their animals, and ready themselves for the final leg of their trip. This road was the only route into Southern California and roughly followed the same route taken in 1775 by Juan Bautista De Anza, who was looking for a path from Tucson to the California Missions. It has been said that upwards of two hundred wagons at one time were camped at the springs.

Even though it is not visited often, Vallecito is still a historic piece of California history.

The lonely Vallecito graveyard, but they do not have to rest alone.

After the army established Fort Yuma in 1850 on the Colorado River to help protect travelers coming west, they established a supply depot at Vallecito to store grain for the animals that had to travel the last one hundred miles across the desert. The soldiers built a warehouse to house and protect the stores. The army maintained this station until 1852 and then abruptly abandoned the site.

In 1853, James R. Lassitor moved his wife and three young step-children to Vallecito and saw a golden business opportunity in the many travelers passing through. Lassitor enlarged the existing warehouse and moved his family into the improved adobe structure. They raised livestock and began selling needed supplies to the travelers, turning the site into a successful store and ranch. After his wife, Sarah, gave birth to a son and then a daughter, Lassitor bought a larger piece of property some miles away and moved his family there, but left his step-son, Andrew, to run the station with help from three other men until the Civil War put a stop to the traffic along the route. Even after the customers stopped arriving, Vallecito continued to operate as a ranch until 1866, when James Lassitor was murdered while on a trip to Arizona.

About the same time that Andrew was taking over operations at the station, the California government was pushing for more dependable communication with Washington back east. In response, the U.S. Congress passed a bill providing for an overland mail route to carry both passengers and mail from Missouri to San Francisco in no more than twenty-five days. James Birch signed a contract to deliver mail between San Antonio and San Diego, but this route only lasted eighteen months, as Birch was killed at sea. This "Jackass Mail," as it became known, did set Vallecito up as a stage stop.

John Butterfield was awarded the contract by Washington to carry the mail from Missouri. After acquiring horses, mules, equipment, men, and stage stops — Vallecito being among them — the first trip left Tipton, Missouri, on September 16, 1858, with John Butterfield's son driving the first leg. To record this historic trip, a reporter from the *New York Herald* named Waterman Ormsby rode along. Most of the stops along the route were designed to change horses and, if needed, drivers. The passengers would get a cold, sparse meal and were back on the trail in only a few minutes. Vallecito was different since it was classified as a "Home Station" and, as such, provided a good hot meal and a spot on the floor for the travelers to sleep. The sleeping accommodations may not have been ideal, but the food was top-notch. Farmers from nearby Palomar provided the produce and meat and the meals consisted of beef stew with fresh-baked bread, fried chicken, and locally-hunted venison.

The Civil War put a stop to all stage traffic along the route and Vallecito changed hands numerous times over the next twenty years; squatters tried to make a go of farming and ranching the area with limited or no success. The last diehards vacated the adobe house and grounds in 1888 and Vallecito sat empty for the next forty-five years. By 1933, the wooden outbuildings had disappeared and the adobe building was almost gone. It seemed that the Vallecito station was destined to vanish into the California desert and become just another lost bit of history in the vast landscape of the American West. In this same year, however, a small group of people realized how important this parcel of land was. Though many miles off any main route, they began the hard work of refurbishing the old derelicts and rebuilding the stage station as it was in its heyday. Their dedication is why Vallecito is a State Historic Landmark and park that we all can enjoy today.

Being from the San Diego area, I have taken my scout troop to Vallecito campground on quite a few occasions. Because of the ghost stories surrounding the stage building, the older scouts like to take the new, younger scouts to this camp in the hopes of giving them a good, fun scare as a sort of an initiation. Until this one night, it had always been in good fun, but now I don't believe we will be going back any time soon.

It was late March and we just had our crossover from Cubs to regular Boy Scouts and decided to again take the younger boys on this camp for a night of campfires and ghost stories. Our Senior Patrol Leader had studied all of the stories surrounding this old stage stop and had come up with some good elaborations to tell everyone once dinner and cleanup was completed. I'll say he did a wonderful job because five of the six new Scouts decided to sleep crammed into a tent designed for two because they were too scared to sleep with less people; the sixth Scout slept with his father that night.

There were four other adult leaders with us on this trip and we stayed up talking with one another until around 11:30 p.m. and then we retired to our individual tents to get some sleep. I hadn't been in my tent for very long when I heard some of the boys talking excitedly about something and was just about to call out for them to quiet down when I noticed another sound. As I was trying to discern what the sound was, one of the boys called out to me and said he was scared. I got out of my tent to go over and let the boys know that there was nothing to fear, but as I walked towards their tent, I realized that I was hearing what sounded like horses coming in our direction. I could not tell exactly which direction it was in, but I became concerned that they were headed straight for our campsite and there was no light to let them know we were here. I quickly made it back to my tent to grab a flashlight and as I turned it on to warn away what sounded now like an entire wagon train bearing down on us, I looked and realized every Scout and leader was outside their tents, looking in the direction that the sound was coming from. We all stood there, mouths open, waiting to see the wagon run our little camp over, but all we saw was the night. As we waited, we did hear the sound of the wagon come into our site, pass by, and then fade from our hearing.

We stood there dumfounded, as we realized that something unbelievable had just occurred. As the leaders of the troop, we began to notice that even our older Scouts were beginning to panic and it took almost three hours to calm all the boys down enough to get them back in their tents. We had to promise them that at least one of us would remain awake the rest of the night, so we took turns in twos, so as to allow us adults a modicum of rest for the long drive home in a few hours. When the sun rose the following day, we looked, but could find no sign of anything going through the camp that night as our SPL said usually happens. We had hoped to get some pictures at least of what we thought we had witnessed, but, unfortunately, all we have is our personal knowledge. Of course, the boys refuse to go back to the camp, but they enjoy telling their friends about how brave they were when the event happened. We see no need to dispute them. What it was that happened that night we won't ever know, but it sounds just like one of the ghost stories that people tell of the area.

~ Benjamin Kennedy

Paranormal Activity

Vallecito Stage Station had its roots in the California gold rush days as the only wagon road into Southern California and because of the lush oasis that grew around its desert spring. It saw its share of tragedy and heartache over the many years of its existence and undoubtedly some of those painful memories still cling to the arid desert floor even today. It is also unusual in that it's a San Diego County Park that has a campground next to a small cemetery and a reportedly haunted replica of a stage station building.

Legend has it that a phantom stagecoach can be heard and seen, usually late at night, pausing briefly at Vallecito and then continuing on before vanishing from sight. The story goes that the stage was carrying a box of gold from El Paso to San Diego. The guard became ill in Yuma, Arizona, and the driver went on unescorted. Somewhere near the Carrizo wash and the nearby station, the stage was heldup by bandits, the driver was killed, and the gold stolen. For some reason, the four mules continued on with the body of their master slumped in his seat, the reins hanging loose in his dead hands. The stage disappeared into the desert and is only seen now as a spectral carriage forever traveling the arid paths of the Anza Borrego Desert. One of the things that seem to make this story more believable is the fact that in the light of day, following the sighting of the stage, mule and wagon tracks have been found and actually photographed by those who witnessed the apparition the night before.

Another story involving spectral animals is that of the White Horse of Vallecito. The story goes that four robbers heldup a stage on its way east. Seeing the bandits' guns drawn, the driver handed over the money box without a fight, but as the men rode away the driver had a change of heart, drew his rifle, and fired. He was rewarded by seeing one of the thieves drop while the others hurried away. When the driver approached the fallen man, he was astonished to find that there were two bandits laying in the sand: the one he had shot and one who had obviously been killed with a pistol. He believed that the crooks were upping their share of the loot by attrition and he had just helped. The other two robbers continued on their way to Vallecito, burying the gold along the way. As one would assume, these greedy men began to argue while having supper at the station. The bandit leader got up and said he would resume the "discussion" when he returned and then left the building. He returned a few moments later, bursting through the door, riding his beautiful white stallion, and shot his partner. As he turned to ride away, the dying man pulled his gun and shot the last robber in the back, killing him. The blast from the gun and the dead man pulling the reins as he fell frightened the horse, which bolted and headed out into the night. It is said that the horse still roams the area where the men buried the gold, waiting for his rider to return. The gold has yet to be found.

Perhaps the most famous ghost story of the area is that of the White Lady of Vallecito. Engaged to be married, her fiancé wanted to make sure he had the means to support his new wife. He traveled to the gold fields of California and told her he would send for her when he had struck it rich. About a year later, the letter arrived, telling her to come to Sacramento, where they would be married as soon as she arrived. The woman immediately bought passage on the stage and headed to meet her love. Just before reaching the Vallecito stop, however, she became deathly ill. She was carried into the station, placed in a bed in the rear room, and was well taken care of over the next few days, but, frail and sick, she succumbed to her illness and died. Going through her luggage, they found her wedding dress and buried her in it. She is one of only three people buried at the Campo Santo Cemetery next to the station; she was placed in an unmarked grave between the two headstones.

It would seem that she was not ready to give up on her life or her fiancé. She is said to still come out every night around dusk and wander about the station grounds, as if searching for something or someone. Some say that her name is Eileen O'Connor. If this is the case, one wonders why she is buried in an unmarked grave. Why would they not inscribe her identity on her marker? This may be a case where legend is not based in fact, but in folklore…merely a tale made up to frighten locals and travelers alike. Whatever the case may be, it is up to you to figure out.

Other tales surrounding the stage area are numerous and include the Phantom Lights of Borrego, which were first reported in 1858 and have been seen near Oriflamme Mountain, Borrego Valley, and other nearby locations. Apparitions include that of a lantern-toting skeleton that is eight feet tall and the Dancing Ghosts of Yaqui Well, along with tales of fireballs that race through the night sky. Planet Paranormal has not rated this site.

The desert around the Vallecito Stage Stop holds many secrets and possibly buried treasure, as well as tales of love, sorrow, kindness, and murder. It holds beauty and grandeur in its stark landscape, but also death to those not prepared for its harshness. Is it any wonder that a place such as this would hold the imagination and spirits of those that have come before? We should be thankful that this oasis in the desert is being kept for future generations to enjoy, so please do check it out for yourself. Remember, though, to be respectful of those who may be watching unseen from the shadows and keep a regard for their surroundings.

VALLECITO STAGE STATION

37349 County Route S-2
858-565-3600
Open: September 1st to May 31st

The "Palace of Your Dreams" as she stands today.

Warner Grand Theatre

The Warner Grand Theatre started out as a way for the Warner brothers to showcase the films coming out of their studios. They planned to build six movie palaces in the lively and growing metropolitan Los Angeles area, but due to the Great Depression in the mid-1930s, only three were ever built: one in Beverly Hills, another in Huntington Park, and the San Pedro Theatre. Of the three, the Warner Grand is the only one still standing as it appeared in 1931 when it opened. The Beverly Hills location was torn down to make way for a parking lot and the Huntington Park movie house was split up to provide space for another venue.

Going to the theater in those early days of the 1930s, when the industry was just coming out with "talkies," was an occasion for women to dress to the nines, for men to put on their Sunday best, and for small boys to don slacks and spit-shined shoes. It was less an evening out and more of a social event, where people were seen and admired by their peers. It was for this reason the Warners spared no expense on their grand movie theaters.

Hired was architect Benjamin Marcus Priteca, who had designed over 150 theaters, including Hollywood's Pantages — the home of the Academy Awards at that time — and the Los Angeles City Hall. Anthony Heinsbergen was brought in to design the murals, bas relief, and structural ornamentation. These two had teamed up on other projects with great success; one good example would be the famous Wiltern Theatre.

The two designed the Warner Grand (Warner Brothers Theatre at that time) in the Art Deco style that was popular at the time. Its sweeping curves, ornate paint schemes, sunburst designs, and lavish fixtures trademarked this style. This beautiful artistry is highlighted at the Warner Grand on the mezzanine and main ceilings. In all, Jack Warner and his two brothers spent a total of $500,000 on the movie palace; that's the equivalent of approximately $5.5 million in modern currency. It has been speculated that if built today the Warner Grand would cost in excess of $50 million. On opening day, January 20, 1931, Jack Warner stood in front of a crowd of movie stars, directors, and their adoring fans and stated, "Here I give you the castle of your dreams!" With those words, Warner opened the box office to his studio's new comic hit *Going Wild*.

Once inside, white-gloved ushers, restroom attendants, and candy girls selling all manner of treats greeted the patrons. There were small acts on stage before the show would begin, from comedians to clowns, and all for the price of 25 cents. The Warner Brothers Theatre became the entertainment hub for the harbor and wouldn't relinquish that title for years to come.

The decline of the grand movie houses can be traced back to the late 1930s, when an anti-trust suit was filed in federal court against the largest studios. Because of their ownership of these theaters, smaller, independent owners were being pushed out of the market. This complaint was settled in 1948 when the studios, including Warner Brothers, agreed to give up ownership.

Once sold, the theater continued running first-rate movies, but ran into trouble as television came on the scene. Movies continued to decline as that form of media improved and then, in the 1960s, the multiplex cinemas began to spring up in malls and shopping centers all over the country, further taking away business from the single-screen venues. In the 1980s, the VCR came on the scene and virtually assured the demise of the once great movie halls. Even the installation of a large 45-foot screen and numerous cutesy gimmicks could not save the Warner from becoming obsolete. Even its designation as a historical and cultural monument had little effect.

The Warner Grand went through many owners in the intervening years and was even a Spanish-language theater named the Teatro Juarez. In this personification, even the seats were redone in a hideous red, green, and gold color scheme. Soon after this incarnation, the movie palace was closed again — and this time demolition seemed to be the next stop.

In 1995, after more than ten years of interest and behind-the-scenes work, a group of preservation-minded fans of the Warner Grand formed the Grand Vision Foundation. In 1996, they incorporated into a 501(c) 3 charity and began enlisting the aid of local and political communities. In that same year, the City of Los Angeles purchased the property and turned it over to the Department of Cultural Affairs.

The Grand Vision's main effort is to raise money for the ongoing restoration of the building to its former glory. Close to a million dollars is needed to fully complete the job. To try to reupholster the seats, they sponsored the "Save Our

Nothing can hide the Warner Grand's art deco beauty.

The Warner Grand, done for the night. All the guests have left...or have they?

Seat" campaign. This was a fund-raiser in which a patron would "buy" a seat for $350 or a block of four for $1,000. The donor would then have their name engraved on a small plaque on the armrest.

The Foundation also hopes to restore a plaque placed when the theater was built honoring Roy A. Moore, the first San Pedro resident killed in World War I. The original was lost over the years and will once again be shown in a place of respect.

In 1999, the grand old theater was added to the National Register of Historical Places, but, again, its future is unclear as the City of Los Angeles faces hard economic times and is looking to close or lease the property. The lease is quite expensive, but the Grand Vision folks are trying to put together a proposal to keep the movies running and the guests coming. We wish them all the luck possible.

I was walking down Sixth Street one night in 1989, coming back from Ports of Call Village, and was just sort of daydreaming as I walked. I remember it was a Thursday, but I can't recall what the time was exactly. I think it was around 10:30 p.m. Anyway, I remember that as I got close to the old Warner Grand Theatre, I could hear music coming from the place. The music sounded like it was the end of a show from the '40s, so I stopped to listen, as I have always loved that style of music. I looked around to see if I was going to be in the way if people started to leave the place, but the theatre looked as if it wasn't even open. The doors were shut; there was no one at the doors or even that many lights on...just the dim lights that are always on at night in downtown.

I stood there listening to this music coming from inside the building, but was slowly starting to realize that the place was, indeed, closed. Just as I was about to move closer to the doors and put my ear up to see if I could hear anybody inside, I was thinking that maybe there was a group practicing for a show. The music stopped and I heard what sounded like the front doors opening. The doors didn't move, but I could clearly hear the sound of a large crowd coming out of the still-closed doors. I saw no one, but could distinctly hear them laughing, talking, and enjoying themselves...and then, just as fast as it started, all the noise stopped. There was no music, no people, no crowd — nothing but the sound of the street noise. The strange part is, I hadn't had a thing to drink all night, but I sure did when I got home.

~ Sam Garcia

Paranormal Activity

The Warner Grand has been reported to have a large amount of ghostly goings-on, so much so that they had been allowing groups to rent the place specifically for the purpose of investigating the paranormal. Because of the budget crisis, it is not certain that will continue. However, that does not mean you cannot go and enjoy a movie or show and check the place out.

Many of the reports go back years. Business owners across the street from the Warner Grand have reported seeing groups of people in 1930s- and '40s-era garb milling about outside and strolling into the theater as if out for a night of movie-going.

Many claim to have seen a man sitting in the back row watching the movie and then he just disappears when the show ends. Speculation of who this may be run the gamut, from the projectionist to Jack Warner himself. Hopefully, someday this movie aficionado's identity will be discovered.

Other spirits have also been seen in the main section of the theater; these apparitions appear to be dressed in all manner and style. It is strange that these moviegoers seem to come together at the same time, even though they are obviously from different time periods. One wonders if they are aware of each other or just exist in their own world of cinema heaven. Orbs are plentiful, if you are into that form of phenomena, and the sound of music can sometimes be heard coming from the now-covered orchestra pit.

One of the most prevalent spirits is that of a former projectionist. Unlike the watcher in the back row, we know this man was, and apparently still is, an employee of the theater. He has been seen loading spectral film into the equipment and even has, on occasion, lent a hand with malfunctioning machines before the viewing audience has had their show interrupted. Jack Warner must be proud of the dedication and devotion to duty shown by this employee. Planet Paranormal rates this site as having mild activity.

The Warner Grand is truly an amazing piece of history in the heart of downtown San Pedro. It stands as a reminder of times when life was simpler and an evening out was spent with the family watching a good old Hollywood musical. Its architecture is magnificent to behold, with its ornate Art Deco style, and brings back those memories of our Saturday matinee heroes. Perhaps our heroes are still there to help entertain you, or perhaps they are waiting in the wings for the chatter of the crowd and the smell of popcorn to once again fill the Grand old Lady of San Pedro with the glitz and hoopla of Hollywood.

WARNER GRAND THEATRE

478 W. 6th Street
San Pedro, CA 90731
310-548-7672

Thomas Whaley built his house in what was then downtown San Diego.

The Whaley House

There are many haunted homes in America. Some are obscure one-room shacks while others are grand mansions; some are famous, most are not — but only one seems to have had a declaration of authenticity signed by the Congress of the United States. I, of course, am speaking of the Whaley House in Old Town, San Diego. This home, built by Thomas Whaley, was home to many generations of Whaleys and now has become a museum dedicated to preserving San Diego's history and lore. To others, however, it has become known for a darker, some say more sinister, reason. It has been declared by Congress to be "the most haunted home in America."

Thomas Whaley came to California from New York in 1849, at the height of the Gold Rush. He was a member of an influential family, whose great-grandfather, a gunsmith, had participated in the Boston Tea Party, had made available his home to George Washington, and provided muskets to the Continental Army during the American Revolution. His father, Thomas, Sr., had carried on in the family business and married Rachel Pye, whose family manufactured locks. Thomas's father also served in the New York Militia during the War of 1812. After the war, Thomas Sr. was taken into the Pye lock business and excelled. About the time that Thomas Jr.

was born, Mr. Whaley established his own holdings by manufacturing engineering and surveying instruments. After his untimely death, the business fell squarely onto the shoulders of his mother. It is under her tutelage that Thomas Jr. learned about real estate and money.

Seeing the way her son took to business, Rachel decided that he should be given the best possible education available. He was sent to boarding school, and after graduation enrolled in the Washington Institute, where he graduated with honors. For the next two years, Thomas went abroad and studied with tutors, traveling through Europe and Spain to see how business affairs were handled outside the United States. Upon his return, he took over the day-to-day operations of the family business until getting a more lucrative job with the shipbuilding firm Sutton & Co.

Just prior to leaving New York, Thomas met a man by the name of George Wardle, who wanted to expand his steamship ventures to the West Coast and asked Whaley to partner with him in the new operation. Thomas quickly agreed and set up a shipment of goods belonging to Wardle, along with locks and guns from his own family's enterprise, to be shipped to San Francisco. Thomas also made this journey on the ship.

Once Thomas arrived, he found the city alive with activity. People wandered the streets, haggling for all kinds of items. It seemed that everyone wanted the fun of the bartering game, seeking the lowest price for the highest quality. Into this maelstrom Whaley set up his shop. As per their agreement, Thomas would receive $600 a month selling Wardle's consignment goods, plus the money from the sale of his own merchandise. He also had arranged for a consignment share from the sale of items from Flintoff & Co. This venture proved quite profitable for Whaley, who earned enough money to open his own two-story storefront. He then rented the Wardle property for $350 a month.

Whaley was beginning to amass the fortune he dreamed of and wrote continuously to his sweetheart, Anne Delaunay. Thomas built a two-story house, where he planned to settle his family, and was just about to write to Anne to tell her to come to California when, in May of 1851, a terrible fire swept through San Francisco, burning at least twenty square blocks and destroying a thousand homes. Soon, more bad news arrived for young Thomas: Anna, still a girl of seventeen, was forbidden by her mother to travel to California to wed Whaley.

Heartbroken, Whaley moved to San Diego to help run the holdings of Lewis Franklin, a friend and business associate. Franklin had already established a small store in the now-labeled Old Town section of San Diego and Thomas found that the climate of Southern California agreed with him. The two men formed a partnership and opened various shops. Whaley began to amass a good deal of money and eventually went out on his own. He learned to speak Spanish to make it easier for him to make transactions with the local populace, and even the specter of a Native American uprising could not dampen his spirits. Writing to his mother in December 1851, he noted, "I am well armed with six shooters and have a horse ready to saddle at a moment's notice." The uprising was all but over by January of 1852, and Thomas

The Whaley House served as the courthouse for the city of San Diego.

The jury is out, or so we think.

was one of twelve men tasked with the ugly job of executing the Native Chief who had started the whole matter.

By now, Lewis Franklin's health was failing and he sold all of the shares that he and Whaley still held together to Thomas. With sales averaging over $150 a day and the stores that he now owned outright doing stellar business, Whaley was determined to go back to New York and wed his sweetheart. They were married August 14, 1853, in New York and then returned to San Diego to a grand ball held at their new place of residence, the Gila House. This was the hotel owned by friend, Juan Bandini, and a temporary home while Thomas looked to buy property for him and his new wife.

Thomas Whaley began construction of his house in September 1856 and it was completed a year later. By this time, Anna had blessed them with two fine sons. This caused Thomas to redesign the home to accommodate his growing family. The *San Diego Herald* dubbed the home "the finest new brick block in Southern California." That same year Whaley opened a general store in the building, but found that it was too far away from the community and had to relocate to a location on the Plaza that he already rented.

On January 29, 1858, Whaley's young son, Thomas III, was found dead just eighteen months after his birth. This devastated both Anna and her husband. In June of that year, their first daughter, Anna Amelia Whaley, was born, which helped to ease, but not erase, the hurt of the death of their son. In August, Whaley was awakened by a pounding at his window and was told that his store in the Plaza was on fire. By the time Thomas arrived, the whole business was completely ablaze and was a total loss. The destruction of his business and the loss of his son was too much for the Whaleys. Together, they decided to move to San Francisco.

Thomas and Anna were quite content in San Francisco and, in March of 1859, Whaley was appointed Commissary Storekeeper to the Presidio. He served in this capacity until 1867, when he was ordered by the Quartermaster to go to Alaska to help set up stores in the new territory there. He was elected to the council of Sitka and raised the first American flag there. Anna and the children would remain in San Francisco to look after the family's interests.

After a major earthquake devastated the Bay area in 1868, Whaley moved his family back to the San Diego home he had built for his wife. There they operated a store out of the home and for a brief time leased out the old courtroom area to the Thomas W. Tanner theatrical troupe. The store was eventually converted into the county courthouse. Over the years this space was also used as a billiards room, kindergarten, Sunday school, dairy, and a residence.

At the time the Whaleys returned to Old Town, "New Town" was beginning to spring up in the south. Alonzo Horton established New Town, San Diego, and the residences of old San Diego were fighting to retain the power of the city there. However, as time went on this was becoming a losing battle. Whaley and his partners could see the writing on the wall and moved their business holdings to New Town, but did not have much success. After the tragic suicide of his daughter Violet in the home by shooting herself, Thomas built a small, single-story on State Street in downtown San Diego and moved his family there. They lived there until his retirement and then death on December 14, 1890.

For the next nineteen years, the old house on San Diego Avenue remained vacant and fell into a state of disrepair. Francis Whaley, seeing the condition of his old home, moved back in that year and began restoration of the old brick building. Thomas's widow, Anna, along with Lillian, Francis, and George, all lived in the house, but Anna would join her husband in death in February 1913 and Francis followed in November 1914.

Lillian would live in the home until her death in 1953, but because of old age and money problems she let the house again fall into disrepair and the home was in danger of being condemned. Supporters of the house stepped in and borrowed money to keep the place from being demolished, hoping to preserve this piece of San Diego's lively past. They began the slow process of trying to raise money for the restoration of the Whaley House, but were having a difficult time of it. In 1956, the County Board of Supervisors stepped in and bought the property with the promise to make the home as it was when Thomas Whaley moved in for the first time with his family.

San Diego is one of my family's favorite spots for weekend getaways. We live in the Los Angeles area and head down to SD to relax and take in the sights such as Sea World for the kids and Old Town for the food and Old World charm. One of the places we like to visit is the Whaley House. We have been there so many times that I have lost count, but the kids always want to go and walk through just so they can look for ghosts.

It was on one of these weekend trips that again the children battered my husband and me into going to the Whaley house, but I opted to stay outside in the garden area while my husband, daughter, and son did their "hunt." Like I said, we have been there so many times that I thought it would be nice to just sit and look at the flowers for a time. The garden is very beautiful and has a section in the back with seats where one can relax, so I staked out a bench where I could look at the windows of the old house and keep an eye out for my family.

I had been sitting there for maybe half an hour and sure enough as I glanced up at one of the second-floor windows I caught a glimpse of my son. I could tell by the look on his face that he was thoroughly enjoying himself. I stared at the window for a few seconds hoping to see my husband and daughter, but my son disappeared into another room, so I went back to contemplating the beautiful yard. As I turned away from the window, I noticed that a woman in period dress had come up and was standing in my little clearing, smiling at me. I thought it odd that I hadn't heard her approach, but figured I had just been too preoccupied with my family to notice.

Looking at her beautiful dress, I figured she was one of the employees of the house and said hello. She smiled and said, "You have a beautiful family." I said thank you and asked if she had kids. "Oh, yes," she said. "They are here with me at the house." As she was obviously an older woman, I smiled and thought to myself how nice it must be for them to all work together. "Family is very important, cherish them," the woman said and then turned to leave. I just smiled and watched her walk away. As I watched, however, I began to notice that she seemed to be dissipating, almost as if she was becoming smoke. Before she had gone more than twenty steps, she simply was not there anymore.

When my husband and children finally came out of the house and joined me in the garden, I was still standing there, looking dumb-founded, and immediately told them what had happened. My husband just smiled, thinking that I was telling a story for my kids until he noticed that my eyes said I was dead serious. The children were, of course, excited and wanted to know everything that had happened and said that they were jealous that I had seen a ghost when they were the ones that were always looking for one. Needless to say, we had plenty to talk about on our trip home to LA.

~ Jessica Allen

Paranormal Activity

There are some human beings who are dimly aware of their own deaths, yet have chosen to stay on in what used to be their homes, to be close to their surroundings that they once held dear. ~ Hans Holtzer

This statement from the renowned paranormalist seems to sum up the Whaley House better than any other statement one could imagine. The haunting activity is said to be so prevalent in this old home that the Congress of the United States has declared the house to be "the most haunted building in the country." If the United States herself has declared this to be true, who am I to dispute it?

One of the first reported occurrences happened not long after the Whaleys moved into the home. Thomas told friends that he heard "heavy footsteps moving about the house." Thomas always believed they were made by James "Yankee Jim" Robinson, a Canadian-born trapper living in San Diego. One night, while drunk, he stole a small fishing boat and went out in the bay for some fun. Upon his return to shore, he was arrested and sentenced to hang. His execution, witnessed by Whaley himself, occurred right at the spot Thomas would later build his home. The hanging was a particularly gruesome one in that Robinson's neck did not snap and he died slowly by strangulation while spectators watched in amusement.

There is some debate over the exact area that Yankee Jim was hanged, with some people saying it was at the spot where the living room arch is positioned today and others claiming that it is where the ninth step of the staircase is located. The latter seems to correspond to reports by many visitors of feeling a choking sensation and being unable to move for an uncomfortably long time. Others have claimed to be pushed at this same step.

Another report says that a young girl is often seen running through the back gardens of the house. This is said to be a neighbor friend of the Whaley children by the name of Carrie or Annabelle Washburn. It is said that the children were playing tag in the backyard and that the Washburn child ran full-force into a clothesline. The line caught her in the neck and essentially strangled her. It is believed that she died in Thomas's arms as he carried her into the house.

This tale may be just that — a tale. No historical record can be found of a little girl having died at the house and no one by the name of Washburn can be found living in San Diego at the time this purportedly occurred. Some speculate this is an urban legend designed to boost the mystique of the haunted reputation of the home.

The cries of a baby have been heard coming from the upstairs bedroom that once belonged to Thomas III. He died at the age of eighteen months from scarlet fever. People have reported getting his image on film, while others report a high number of orbs being captured in that same room.

Anna Whaley has been seen strolling through the gardens of the house and even appeared to television host Regis Philbin. Anna is usually spotted in the downstairs parlor and has been known to like the piano. Other areas where she has been seen are the kitchen and even in the courtroom. She is most often seen looking out of one of the upstairs windows. One can never tell where she may be gazing or at what, but keep your eyes open when looking at the house from outside.

Thomas makes himself known by the smell of his cigar. The odor can be perceived from anywhere in the house, indicating that Thomas still looks after his residence. He has been seen most on the upstairs landing, wearing a wide brim hat and long coat. He stares for a minute and then fades away, leaving visitors to wonder about their eyesight. He has also been seen in the courthouse, where it is believed he makes objects move and may even rearrange the chairs.

There have been reports over the years by many of the docents of the pillows and beds appearing to have an imprint of a body laying down as if someone is sleeping. Footsteps have also been heard both on the second floor and in the parlor, as well as the courtroom and also going up and down the staircase. The sound of children's laughter and playing have been reported in the gardens and from the children's bedrooms. Even the family terrier has been seen and heard haunting the old house.

Thomas Whaley embodies the pioneer spirit that built this great nation and his business acumen helped not only build the Alaska Territory, but also helped establish San Diego as a world-class modern city. His house still stands as a testimony to his rugged individualism and vision. Building his residence on the site of so many public hangings may have been one of the reasons his longest surviving daughter never felt comfortable living alone for so long in the family home. The tragic deaths of his son and daughter in the house may be another reason it is so haunted. Planet Paranormal rates the Whaley House as moderate to high paranormal activity.

Check out this place for yourself and see this piece of history, this place of both death and family...but be careful not to disturb its former residents. Make no mistake about it, though: Thomas Whaley and his wife are still there, looking after the place and making sure it is cared for properly. How do I know this? Because the United States says it's so.

THE WHALEY HOUSE

2476 San Diego Avenue
San Diego, CA 92110
619-297-7511
soho-1@sohosandiego.org

Central California

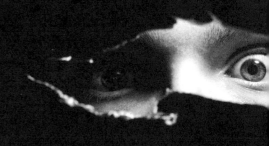

The Calico schoolhouse has had its share of ghostly tales.

Calico Ghost Town

Located in the Mojave Desert, about fifteen miles northeast of the town of Barstow, California, sits a true gem of Wild West history. We know this nugget of mining lore as Calico Ghost Town.

The town began in 1881 when, in April of that year, S. C. Warden, Hues Thomas, Charlie Mecham, and John C. King laid claim to ore strikes on Calico Mountain (named for the mottled color of the rocks). They named their claim the Silver King Mine. As often happens, word of the strike reached the ears of other fortune seekers and they moved into the area below the Silver King and a town started to grow. By spring of 1882, one hundred people lived in the town and no less than forty-six mines were operating. The most profitable of these were the Burning Moscow, Oriental, Waterloo, Bismark, and Garfield, along with the Silver King. In July of 1882, the Silver King was sold to a corporation from San Francisco for $300,000, quite a tidy sum in that period. Numerous mills that sprang up in the area processed the ores from these mines. In all, almost five hundred mines sprang up in the hills around Calico.

Initially, the ore was moved from the mines to Oro Grande, some forty miles distant, but in late 1882 a stamp mill was built in the town of Daggett, which sat along the Mojave River. This mill had ten stamps (upgraded to fifteen in 1884), which, at that time, could more than accommodate the ore load coming out of the hills. There were other mills in the area: at Camp Cady, one near Mule Canyon, and another located at the mouth of Odessa Canyon. At first, the ore was transported by wagon, but in 1888 a small, narrow gauge railroad was built, which drastically reduced the cost of shipping to the mills.

Calico had one street that sat on an incline, had very little water, and the temperatures would range from extremes of 120 degrees in the summer to nights well into freezing in the winter. It took a hearty soul to live and survive in these conditions and those facing death on a daily basis were wont to be a bit boisterous. Calico had twenty-two saloons, numerous bordellos, restaurants, boarding houses, and flop shacks to serve the needs of its 1,200 citizens. One of its more colorful inhabitants was a dog by the name of Dorsey. This amazing collie became the mail carrier for the town. As told, the human mailman for Calico became ill one day and Dorsey, having traveled the route many times with his owner, had a paper rubbed across his nose and was told to deliver the parcels. The dog did a fair job with this over the next couple of mail days, which convinced his master to give him the job full-time. Dorsey became so famous over the intervening years that a news story was written about him, which brought him even more fame.

The town burned to the ground in the fall of 1883 and was promptly rebuilt, this time with the addition of a Chinatown. This part of town was added due to the influx of Chinese immigrants brought in to construct the narrow gauge railroad being built to make it easier to transport the raw ore from the mines to the various processing mills.

In 1890, the price of silver dropped dramatically and the town began to decline in both residents and prosperity. The discovery of borate in 1883 saved the town and helped keep it alive. The silver mines continued to turn out ore, but it became too costly for them to operate and in 1892 all but one of the major operations shut down. The last, the Silver King, managed to hold out until 1896, when it, too, ceased to operate. Many smaller operations continued, but the silver glory days of Calico were at an end. From 1881 to 1892, Calico's mines churned out $13 to $20 million worth of raw silver ore. The borax mines continued to operate until 1907 after producing more than $9 million of the mineral.

The town still would not die, however, and a few hearty souls stayed to keep Calico going. In 1917, a small group of investors arrived and started using the cyanide process to extract the low-grade silver from the Silver King trailings. This produced modest results and barely paid for the cost of extraction. In the 1930s, the Zenda Gold Mining Company opened a small operation to mine silver, and from 1930 to 1941, gold was mined from the Total Wreck Mine. By 1950, though, with the mining operations over and the town in decay, Calico was virtually deserted. Only Mrs. Lucy Bell Lane remained — Calico was her home and nothing and no

Calico Ghost Town is a gem in the Mojave Desert.

The ground at the Calico cemetery is hard and dry, but still shows signs of recent burials.

Named for the mottled color of the mountain rocks, Calico has made a name for itself.

The mining town today welcomes everyone with open arms.

one would drive her away. She would live there until her death in 1960; today, her house is home to the Calico town museum.

As a young man in the early 1900s, Walter Knott lived and mined Calico for a summer to earn extra money. The experience stayed with him into adulthood and, in 1950, hearing of the town's plight and in the market for a hook to draw visitors to his wife's chicken restaurant in Buena Park, California, Walter Knott purchased the town of Calico. He moved some of the buildings from Calico to the area next to her business and that laid the foundation for his now famous theme park, Knott's Berry Farm.

Residents living nearby were not happy with the fact that Walter was dismantling such an important piece of the area's history and let him know that they wanted him to stop. Mr. Knott, however, was already in the process of gathering old photos and records in an effort to begin restoration. His idea was to make the town a living part of gold mining history. Only five of the original buildings remain, but Knott did such a good job of aging the new structures that it's hard to tell which of these are the new buildings and which are the old. Many of the new buildings were recreated on the original foundations, but others, such as the mystery shack, are pure imaginative entertainment. What Knott created was a place where people could go to get a glimpse of what it was like to live and work in the gold rush days, but also a place where you could be entertained and amazed.

In 1966, with the restoration complete, Walter Knott began the process of donating the town to the County of San Bernardino. The county added a campground, cabins, and a guest bunkhouse, and operates the town today as the tourist attraction that Mr. Knott had envisioned. Visitors can enjoy gunfight stunt shows, a mine tour, the Calico & Odessa narrow gauge railroad, restaurants, burger stands, and many varied and unique shops.

I was with my Scout troop and we had just finished cleaning up after dinner when our older patrol said they wanted to go and explore the cemetery. I was a bit leery of them doing this, as I knew that the town Rangers frowned upon anyone wandering around town at night. It was only about 8 p.m. and I told them that it would be okay, but only if I was with them. They were a bit disappointed in having an adult along, but the Scout Master agreed that an adult must be with them since it was dark and a bit away from where we were camped.

We gathered up our flashlights and started the long walk to the cemetery. We ran into one of the Rangers along the way who told us that if we wanted to check out the cemetery it was okay — but if he saw us inside the walls he would throw us and the rest of the troop out of the camp. We agreed that we would not try to actually go inside and this further dampened the boys' spirits about doing their "ghost hunt," as they were calling it, but as we were already most of the way there we continued on.

The wind was gusting a bit and as we made our way up the hill we could hear the iron gate creaking and making eerie noises, which made the boys giggle. I could tell it set the mood for them nicely, as the closer we got, the more they seemed to get into the spirit of the hunt. Once we got to the main gate of the cemetery, we just stood there, looking through the iron bars and listening to the gate squeal. Neither myself nor any of the Scouts had ever done anything like this before, so we weren't really sure what to do. After awhile, one of the boys suggested we try to walk along the outside of the wall and see what we could find. I told them that as long as they were careful we could give it a try, but if it became in any way dangerous we would have to turn back. They agreed and we headed out.

As we walked along the perimeter of the cemetery, I thought I could hear talking, like a very low whisper, coming from inside the wall. I couldn't make out what was being said and figured it was just a combination of my imagination and the blowing wind. The further we walked toward the opposite side of the cemetery, however, the louder it became and I heard the boys talking about hearing a voice also. I knew that there were quite a few other groups camping and staying in the cabins on site and was concerned that there were other people in the cemetery that might cause the Rangers or us problems. I told the boys that we should probably head back the way we came, but one of the Scouts pointed out that it was just as close to continue from where we were as it was to go back…and I reluctantly agreed to go on.

We had just passed what I figured was the exact opposite area across from the gate when we all heard a very loud "What are you doing here?", which seemed to come from inside the cemetery. We all stopped to look to see who was questioning us and, figuring it was a Ranger, I was prepared to tell him that the Ranger who stopped us earlier had said it was okay. None of us could see anyone from where the voice had come. We stood there a second and then started moving forward again. As soon as we were on the move, the voice again said, "I said what are you doing here?" We stopped again and this time when we looked toward the cemetery we all could see what appeared to be a person materialize right out of thin air. The boys all screamed and I just yelled, "Run!", and we bolted as fast as we could back to the campground.

~ Lewis Bush

Paranormal Activity

The Calico schoolhouse is probably the most famous haunted location in town. It is not one of the original buildings, but was constructed to exact dimensions using old photos and records. Its spirit is thought to be the old schoolmarm, Virginia Merritt. She sometimes appears inside the classroom and a British couple swears they took pictures with her and had a long conversation about the "old days" in the town thinking she was a re-enactor. They say that when they returned home and had the pictures developed, the "staff member" did not appear in any of the photos. They later found out that there was no one employed at the town in that capacity.

The Maggie Mine is another spot where people believe spirits dwell. While the mine was in operation, the Mulcahey brothers dug out an area large enough for the two of them to live in across from one of the small "glory holes"; at this spot people have reported being lightly pushed, as if being told to move along. They also say they smell cooking and the hair on their arms and neck suddenly stand up. The "Y" in the shaft also gets cold spots that pop up and seem to move to different locations nearby. Not much of this mine is open to the public, but these stories make one wonder what else lurks deeper in the tunnels.

The cemetery may not be one of the more talked about areas of spirit activity; however, when Planet Paranormal investigated this site, we caught our only small bit of evidence from the town in the form of an EVP. In a town of over 1,200 people, it is hard to believe that only forty should be buried in its cemetery. It is conceivable that when Walter Knott had the wall built around these graves he did not realize that there were other, unmarked graves in the area… If you wander around that area, please be aware of this and be respectful of what may be under your feet.

The hotel in Calico is now an artist's studio. Reports of phantom odors and the sounds of footsteps are common from the artists who ply their craft in the building. There have even been stories of tourists who have seen people looking from the windows wearing period clothing. This is not one of the original buildings, but maybe the "guests" don't seem to realize this fact.

There is an area next to the upper parking lot that may have been used as a site for cremations by the local Asian population. This area is said to have high incidents of orb activity and cold spots. This is an outside location and that should be taken into account when investigating here.

One of the employees of the current candy shop tells of an entity that appears there on occasion and the building that now houses the fossil shop (formerly the town theater) has also had an apparition spotted within its walls. The actors that used to perform there have reported items and props would disappear from where they were set down, only to appear somewhere else in the building.

Most of the Ranger staff at Calico, like others, seem to have a disdain of anything having to do with the paranormal, including those who research the subject. Keep this in mind when you go and be respectful of their views. Planet Paranormal rates Calico as having moderate activity.

Calico truly is a gem in the desert. It is a living history lesson in the art of mining and a snapshot of life as it may have been in California in the late 1800s. Walter Knott went to great lengths to preserve and rebuild the town and the county has continued to keep alive the spirit of the place. Today, a family can stay in the on-site campground and rent one of the many small cabins; even groups can rent the bunkhouse. There are things here to please everyone, from the grandparents to the kids. The atmosphere is that of an old friend. Who knows, you may even make one...one who may be even older than you expect.

CALICO GHOST TOWN

36600 Ghost Town Road
Yermo, CA 92398
1-800-TO-CALICO
www.sdcountyparks.com
www.calicotown.com

Visitor Information

Daily admission:

$8 for adults; $5 for children ages 6 to 15; free for children under 5

Camping fees:

Site with no hookups are $30 a night; partial hookup $34; full hookup $35 a night;

Cabins are $45 a night (deposit required);

Bunkhouse is $80 (maximum 20 people)

Mini-bunkhouse is $100 and sleeps 6 with a kitchenette and private bathroom and shower (deposits required for bunkhouses)

La Purisima's bells once rang out, calling the faithful and the Chumash Indians to mass.

La Purisima Mission

The mission was established December 8, 1787, by Father Ferman Lasuen. Today, however, La Purisima Mission sits on a different plot of land from that of the original complex. This is due to a series of earthquakes that shook the area on December 8, 1812, twenty-five years after it was founded. The earthquakes were bad enough, but the rains that followed were prolonged and the unprotected adobe bricks could not stand up to the pelting and disappeared back into the earth. This area was abandoned and the new mission was rebuilt on the opposite side of the Santa Inez River, in a small canyon that the Chumash people called Amuu and the Spaniards named La Canada de Los Berros (canyon of the watercress).

This new site offered many advantages that the old site lacked. The ground was much more level, there were more trees that could be used for building and firewood, there was a more abundant supply of material used for construction, acreage for farmland, and direct access to the El Camino Real, which was the only road connecting the California missions — and so, on April 23, 1813, La Purisima Mission was officially established on the site we visit today.

Construction of the new mission began immediately using many salvaged materials from the original site. The new complex was a radical departure in design

The fire ring at La Purisima is known to have spectral Chumash celebrations that can be seen by some visitors.

This marker in the altar area shows where Father Payeras rests.

FR. MARIANO PAYERAS OFM
NACIO EN MALLORCA 1769,
FALLECIO AQUI 28 DE ABRIL
1823

PREDICADOR APOSTOLICO DEL COLECIO
DE SAN FERNANDO DE MEXICO
MISIONERO DE ESTA MISION
PREFECTO DE TODAS LAS MISIONES
DE ALTA CALIFORNIA

REQUIESCAT IN PACE

Rangers who open the mission in the morning often report that the bed in this room looks slept in — with the covers pulled down and the pillow ruffled.

from the rest of the missions in the system, in that the buildings were laid out in a straight line along the base of the hills rather than the traditional box layout. This was done to allow the residents to escape from the buildings in case of more earthquakes and to keep from encroaching onto the farmland nearby. Under the guidance of Padre Payeras, it took only ten years to construct the buildings, including the church. Today, all of the buildings remain at La Purisima State Park.

In 1815, Padre Payeras was made head of the mission system and was ordered to the Carmel Mission that was the traditional residence of the mission head. He refused. For four years, Father Payeras directed the California missions from La Purisima and then, in 1819, he was again honored with the promotion to President and was appointed Commissary Prefect, the highest office of the California Franciscans. During his tenure, Padre Payeras worked tirelessly to provide supplies to the surrounding settlements, having realized that they — the missions and presidios — were interdependent on each other. This became increasingly more difficult because of the Hidalgo Rebellion in Mexico and the strain it was putting on Spain's resources and shipping. By 1811, the supplies ceased altogether, along with the $1,000 stipend for the mission. It was not allowed in California at that time to trade with foreign merchants and this caused a shortage in needed goods, such as clothes, farm equipment, and candles for light. On the other hand, the Chumash now had a surplus of hides and other items that could be used. A black market soon developed, which bred animosity between the military and the mission population. The strain of all this wore on Father Payeras and his body finally quit on April 28, 1823. He was buried under the altar in the main church at La Purisima and to this day is the only Padre so honored in the Mission system.

The soldiers were becoming poverty-stricken and became totally dependent on the missions for their support; the frustration of this was taken out on the mission Indians. The Neophytes (Christianized Native Americans) were used for military construction, but were paid little or nothing. In 1822, Mexico won independence and Spain's support of the mission system vanished. The hope that the missions could recover the hundreds of thousands of dollars loaned to the King in the form of goods and supplies vanished with the supply ships.

In early 1824, the friction between the soldiers and the Chumash reached a boiling point when a neophyte was flogged at the Santa Inez Mission. The news spread to the other two Santa Barbara missions and the Chumash rose up in revolt. At La Purisima, the Chumash immediately took control of the mission grounds, but allowed the soldiers and their families to go to Mission Santa Inez and Padre Ordaz went with them. Father Rodriguez stayed to try to calm the situation and was given reign to come and go as he pleased.

When the Governor of California heard about the uprising, he commissioned Lieutenant Estrada to take a force of 109 men from the presidio to quell the hostilities. It took a couple of weeks to reach La Purisima and then a nearly three-hour battle in which sixteen Chumash were killed and many more were wounded. Of the 110 Spaniards, only one died and two were wounded. Father Rodriquez was able to reach terms of surrender; however, the Governor was determined to make an example out of the Chumash. He sentenced seven to death for the killing of four Spanish travelers during the occupation the first night, with twelve others given hard labor at the presidio. As a note, one of the travelers killed was Jose Delores Sepulveda, a central figure in the development of early California history.

Life at the missions returned to normal with the Chumash doing the work and the Spaniards reaping the moderate rewards. The native culture and heritage was being erased as they became more "civilized" and they became used to the Padres guiding and protecting them and then, in 1834, Governor Jose Figueroa completely secularized the mission system.

When the secularization began, the Padres of the three Santa Barbara Missions were all transferred to Santa Inez and the mission lands, including those at La Purisima, were divided up among the neophytes, with each also receiving seed, livestock, and equipment to start their own ranch. They would also continue to operate the old mission shops, storehouses, and supplies under the direction of a new Mayordomo who was appointed by the Governor.

The Spaniards still would not allow the Chumash to farm or run the shops for the benefit of themselves, but were required to fill the orders of grain, wool, shoes, tack, and other needs of the military and their families. This led to despair among the Chumash, who began to leave the pueblos in search of a better life, free of the meddling of the Spaniards. Within ten years, the mission, once in a sharp state of decay, had all but disappeared.

I have always heard that the La Purisima Mission was ragingly haunted, so when a friend invited me along for his group's investigation of the site I was more than happy to say yes. We got there early in the day, checked into our hotel, and then headed to the Mission to scout it out for our investigation later that night. I found the place to be fascinating even during the day. The history of the place just oozed out of the walls and I could feel, even then, the presence of quite a few ghosts, both Chumash and Spanish alike.

We wandered around the outside of the buildings, cemetery, village site, and hallways, trying to get a feel for the place. Because we would be unable to enter any of the buildings once the park closed and our group assembled, we decided to do an informal investigation of the church and some of the other buildings. Unfortunately, this impromptu ghost hunt netted no results, other than some minor personal stuff. That would not be the case later on, though.

We went back into town and had a light dinner and short nap. We headed out to the investigation around 6 p.m. The night started out slow because we had about 25 people present and it took some time to break us into four groups.

We would each take an area to investigate for an hour and then rotate to the next area; after we investigated all the areas, we would then gather together and talk about what occurred and what we found.

The first stop for my group was the cemetery. After walking around the area for a few minutes taking pictures and getting a feel for the place, we settled in to do an EVP session; this was repeated in the other areas as well, but it was in the Chumash Village site that we all got more than we expected. It was the third area for my group to investigate and we pretty much did the same as the other two areas before it, which is walk around to get the feeling and to snap some pictures. I noticed as soon as I entered the site that we were going to get a lot of activity because I could feel the ghosts milling about and their curiosity building as to why we were there. It didn't take long once we started our recording session for things to start happening.

Jerry started our EVP group off with our standard mundane questions of why are you here, how many of you are here, why do you stay here, and so forth, and then it was my turn to ask a few questions. I started by asking the group of ghosts if they were Indians and I immediately noticed a flash of light come from the old fire pit. I took this as a yes and continued my questions from the point knowing I was talking to the Chumash. During my questioning, I led the conversation to life at the village and what the people did for fun. As soon as I asked this, I noticed a light starting to emanate from the fire pit and began hearing the faint sound of drums. As I watched the pit, the light and the drums grew and it wasn't long before figures started to appear around the fire. These figures seemed to be dancing to the beat of the drums and I soon realized that the Tribesman were showing me one of their most sacred dances. I felt so gratified that they would trust me with this knowledge that I began to cry. Seeing me in tears, Jerry asked what was wrong and if I was okay. I asked him if the music and dance stirred anything within him and he just said, "What music? What are you talking about?" As soon as Jerry said this, it all stopped — the music, the fire, and the ghosts were gone.

As my eyes readjusted to the darkness, I started to notice everyone in the group was staring at me. They all wanted to know why I was crying and what I had seen. I related what I had witnessed and how privileged I felt to have been brought into the tribe in that way. Many in the group looked skeptical, but many others looked at me with awe and respect. For those that doubt me about what occurred, I can only say that I know I was touched by the Chumash that night and I will always be a part of them now — they will always be a part of me. It is my truth and I know it to be such.

~ Margaret Booth

In 1845, the state decided to divest itself of the former mission and a public auction was held. John Temple was the highest bidder and La Purisima passed into his hands. Not much is known about what the land was used for, although it is speculated that Mr. Temple planned to use the area for farming. What is known is that the adobe buildings fell into ruin and, by 1903, the year Union Oil acquired the land, only nine remained standing and those were in danger of complete collapse. The Union Oil Company, recognizing the historical importance of the property, deeded the site and the surrounding area to Santa Barbara County for restoration in 1933.

In 1934, the first Civilian Conservation Corps (CCC) crews arrived. Their first order of business was to gather as much historical information as possible. They scoured any written records that could be found on the mission and an archeological dig uncovered thirteen building ruins. These findings provided the information needed to restore the adobe structures using techniques similar to those used by the padres and Chumash in the original construction. By the time the mission was dedicated on December 7, 1941, as a State Historical Monument, only three buildings were complete and the walls of three smaller ones were erected. Over the years the smaller buildings were completed and additional structures reconstructed, making La Purisima the most complete of the twenty-one California Missions. Even today, it is the only example of a complete complex in the mission system. The restoration was completed in 1951.

In 1973, a major step was taken by the Department of Parks and Recreation when it established a five-member group known as Prelado de los Tesoros de la Purisima (The Keepers of the Treasures of La Purisima). These volunteers are dedicated to preserving the heritage and history of Mission La Purisima Concepcion de Maria Santisima (The Immaculate Conception of Mary the Most Pure).

Today, the Mission is a tourist attraction and classroom, complete with a visitor's center and guided tours. Visitors can watch reenactments, from grinding corn with authentic native tools to sheep being sheared, learning how to weave and spin cloth, and seeing an actual Chumash village and how life was in the mission system.

Paranormal Activity

Over the years many people have reported strange and inexplicable occurrences at La Purisima. It is not hard to believe that with everything that has happened on the mission grounds there could still be spirits lurking about, wanting to have their story told. The populations of the missions were treated like slaves: they worked long hours, were not allowed to leave the compounds, and were forced to give up their heritage and religion in favor of the new Christian order. The Europeans brought sickness with them that the Chumash had no natural immunity against, which caused countless deaths over the years. The Spanish soldiers repeatedly abused the Chumash, accusing them of false crimes due to their bigotry towards the native people of California. This led to unrest and rebellion, which caused even more deaths to not only the Chumash, but to some Spaniards as well.

Cold spots are a common occurrence all over the grounds, though they are felt mostly in the church and cemetery areas. Also in the chapel, people have heard singing and the sounds of a flute playing softly. The flute was a favored instrument of the Chumash neophytes. In and around the Chumash village area, the sounds of native chanting, accompanied by the staccato tapping of drums, has been heard and the hoofbeat sounds of spectral horses can be caught after dark. There have been reports of the apparitions of padres and monks wandering the halls and rooms of the mission buildings still going about their daily chores.

Tour guides and park rangers have all reported seeing wispy, insubstantial shapes and hearing whispers near them while at the same time feeling cold drafts that seem to float by and then disappear. Phantom children, believed to be those who had died from a smallpox epidemic, were seen by members of the CCC when the renovation was taking place. Padre Mariano Payeras has been seen numerous times in the chapel near where his body is entombed. It is said that if you stand on his grave out of disrespect, bad luck shall follow you. Murdered more than 150 years ago Don Vicente still haunts the kitchen and even a ghostly groundskeeper has been seen still tending to the mission's grounds. We consider La Purisima to have moderate activity.

With fires, earthquakes, flooding, murder, and riots, is it any wonder that La Purisima would have a large number of restless spirits still roaming its pristine grounds? For those of you looking for proof of the afterlife, this piece of California history should satisfy your craving. For those of you who enjoy history or Spanish-style architecture, then please go see this jewel in Santa Barbara County. Remember, though: the grounds are also those of a sacred nature and if one acts with disrespect, then beware…for you will not only anger the spirits of those padres and soldiers who administered there, but also the Chumash, who built the buildings and suffered, bled, and were killed there.

LA PURISIMA MISSION

2295 Purisima Road
Lompoc, CA 93436
805-733-3713
www.lapurisimamission.org

Nestled far off the highway and atop a picturesque ocean cliff, Moss Beach Distillery is well worth the travel.

Moss Beach Distillery

Located on California's central coast, Moss Beach is one of those places where beauty seeps from the very fabric of the land and a sense of calm greets visitors as they gaze towards the shoreline. One would never dream that a place as lovely as this would harbor a dark and deadly secret from the past — a secret of lust, crime, and betrayal.

Juergen F. Wienke was a farmer and mining engineer in Germany, but he thought the opportunities in the United States would be better than his current lot, so he boarded a ship and headed to San Francisco. He did odd jobs for a while, some of which were in the service industry, where he learned that there was a need to cater to the rich and affluent and thought that he might try his hand at this by buying his own hotel.

Wienke was fond of exploring the coastline and found a wonderful secluded little town south of San Francisco that he immediately fell in love with. When he learned that there were plans to build a railroad between Santa Cruz and San Francisco and that this quaint beach community was along the route, he decided this would be a good place to start his dream. The family that owned the land was in financial trouble and jumped at the opportunity to get out from under their debt, so, in 1881, Francisco Guerrero sold his entire property and Moss Beach was born.

The Blue Lady is often seen staring out to sea from this prominent cliff top.

The men's bathroom seems to be a favorite haunt of the Blue Lady.

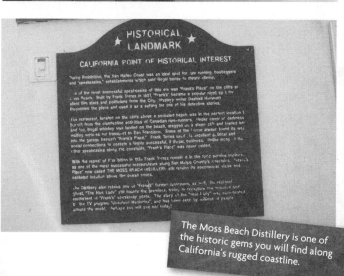

★ HISTORICAL ★
LANDMARK

CALIFORNIA POINT OF HISTORICAL INTEREST

During Prohibition, the San Mateo Coast was an ideal spot for rum-running, bootleggers and "speakeasies," establishments which sold illegal booze to thirsty clients.

One of the most successful speakeasies of this era was "Frank's Place" on the cliffs at Moss Beach. Built by Frank Torres in 1927, "Frank's" became a popular night spot for silent film stars and politicians from the City. Mystery writer Dashiell Hammett frequented the place and used it as a setting for one of his detective stories.

The restaurant, located on the cliffs above a secluded beach was in the perfect location to benefit from the clandestine activities of Canadian rum-runners. Under cover of darkness and fog, illegal whiskey was landed on the beach, dragged up a steep cliff and loaded into waiting vehicles for transport to San Francisco. Some of the liquor always found its way into the garage beneath "Frank's Place." Frank Torres used his excellent political and social connections to operate a highly successful, if illegal, business. Unlike many of the other speakeasies along the coastside, "Frank's Place" was never raided.

With the repeal of Prohibition in 1933 Frank Torres remained in the food service business, as one of the most successful restaurateurs along San Mateo County's coastside. "Frank's Place" now called THE MOSS BEACH DISTILLERY still retains its spectacular views and secluded location above the ocean coves.

The Distillery also retains one of "Frank's" former customers, as well. Its resident ghost, "The Blue Lady" still haunts the premises, trying to recapture the romance and excitement of "Frank's" speakeasy years. The story of the "Blue Lady" was dramatized in the TV program "Unsolved Mysteries," and has been seen by millions of people around the world. Perhaps you will see her today!

The Moss Beach Distillery is one of the historic gems you will find along California's rugged coastline.

123

Legend has it that Wienke, seeing the algae growing on the rocks along the beach, thought it was moss and called the place by the name we know it by today.

It took only a year to build the Moss Beach Hotel and Juergen spared no expense in creating his "spa and health" resort. He spent a good amount of time over that year publicizing his vacation oasis to the city elite and his hard work paid off with an overflow of bookings. At that time, the only way to reach Moss Beach was by stage over a perilous stretch of road known as Devil's Slide, but once the Ocean Shore Railroad was built the rich and famous flocked to the area.

Over time, the town grew and businesses were built to take advantage of Wienke's success. The Reefs Restaurant went up on the dunes and became as famous for its seafood as the Moss Beach Hotel was for its hospitality, but in 1911 disaster struck. A fire spread through the hotel and burned it to the ground. Wienke, although still enamored with his town, decided not to rebuild. Juergen Wienke would go on to become a beloved mayor and city leader. The Reefs would eventually be destroyed by the pounding surf, but would be rebuilt and then it, too, would be destroyed again.

Moss Beach would gain its most everlasting fame during the Prohibition days. The Roadhouse was built in 1917 and became a popular hangout for the Hollywood crowd, as well as powerful politicians of the day. It was so popular that a hotel was built next door, so that those who were too inebriated to make it home had a safe place to sleep it off.

When Prohibition took effect on January 17, 1920, the Roadhouse scarcely missed a beat. Because of the secluded, oftentimes fog-shrouded coves, the area around Moss Beach became a prime spot for bootleggers to smuggle in their illegal alcohol. Because the bar patrons were rich and famous as well as powerful civic leaders, the police would look the other way or they would become customers themselves. Seal Cove, directly below the speakeasy, became the main drop off point for Canadian whisky coming into San Francisco and the bar reaped the benefits by paying cheap prices for the bottles.

In 1927, Frank Torres purchased the speakeasy and renamed it Frank's Roadhouse and later just Frank's Place. Torres did well enough with the bar to also buy the hotel next door and became a prominent figure in the area. Even into death Frank Torres swore he never bought illicit alcohol, but considering he owned the bar for two years before the 18th amendment was repealed one must make their peace with this bit of knowledge.

Many famous people passed through the doors of the Roadhouse; names such as Fatty Arbuckle, Gloria Swanson, Rudolph Valentino, and Dashiell Hammett. Hammett, it is said, was so taken with the place that he used the speakeasy in one of his books.

Frank's Roadhouse went through many changes along the way to becoming the Moss Beach Distillery. The Marina View Hotel next door burned down in 1958 and the tourist traffic slowly began to fade, but the old speakeasy endured and today is one of the finest restaurants along the California coast.

My husband and I had driven down from Portland, Oregon, for a romantic weekend in Monterey and had made reservations to have dinner at the Moss Beach Restaurant, which we had heard was very good. We thought that it was a rather strange location for a fancy restaurant as we drove up, but once inside we were pleasantly surprised.

We had arrived a little ahead of schedule, so we took some seats at the bar and ordered a couple of drinks to enjoy while we waited for our table. As we sat there, my husband noticed that the light fixtures seemed to move every once in awhile, so we asked the bartender what was going on. He told us the place was haunted and the moving lights were just a fun way of reminding guests about that fact. My husband and I then started to recall the tales of the place. We remembered hearing about a love triangle — that a young woman had died because of this affair — and something about the mob being involved, but beyond this we couldn't really recall what had transpired. This fact about the restaurant made it seem even more exiting of a night out.

We had been sitting at the bar for about 40 minutes when our waitress came to take us to our table. The table we were given was right against the window that overlooked the cliffs and ocean. I remember thinking to myself how lucky we were to get this table. The whole time I was trying to decide what I would have for dinner I was thinking about how I would love to walk along the cliff with my husband…about how much I loved him. After we ordered our dinner, as we were sipping our wine, my husband and I scarcely said a word. We were looking into each other's eyes in a way that we hadn't in years. I don't know if it was the location, the sunset, or the fact that we were in a romantic mood, all I know is that the feeling we shared was something I had longed to feel for a long time. It was becoming the perfect night.

Dinner was wonderful and dessert was even better. We ordered a couple of nightcaps before heading back to our hotel and asked the waitress if it would be okay to stand outside on the lower patio, which was closed at the time, to drink them? She told us that would be fine, so we headed downstairs and out onto the breezy patio. It was a pleasant night and we were in no hurry to leave this lovely spot, so we just sat sipping our drinks and enjoying each other's company.

My husband noticed there was someone out on the cliffs and wondered if it could be dangerous because the woman seemed to be wearing a long gown. We were about to call out when the woman appeared to just leap off the cliff right in front of us. Horrified, we rushed back into the restaurant to get someone to call 911, but when we explained to the hostess what had occurred, she just smiled and said, "Don't worry... that's just the Blue Lady. She does that every once in a while." We just stared at her wondering what was wrong with her and why she wasn't calling the police. I guess she saw the concern still on our faces and explained that the Blue Lady had been dead for close to 100 years and is sometimes spotted on the cliffs. She then handed us a piece of paper with the story of the ghosts that are seen in the area and told us not to worry and that we now had a great story to tell our friends.

~ Margery Stanley

Paranormal Activity

As I stated at the beginning of this chapter, the Moss Beach Distillery has had its brush with the darker side of human behavior. During the Prohibition era, organized crime was the sole supplier of booze to the San Francisco area. With that came all of the baggage and elements one would associate with the mob. Speakeasies, for their part, regardless of upscale clientele, brought with them an air of lawlessness that would seep into a person and, mixed with alcohol, could change the character of that individual, most times for the worse.

This mix of circumstances may be the catalyst for a love story as tragic as any told by the bard and one that won't die...just as the victim won't admit that she is dead. I am speaking, of course, of the famous Blue Lady of Moss Beach. There are at least two versions of this unfortunate love story depending on with whom you speak, but they both end in the violent death of a beautiful woman and her inability to pass on.

Legend has it that a young woman by the name of Mary Ellen (others believe her name to be Elizabeth Claire Donovan) who liked to frequent the speakeasy sometime in the 1920s met and fell in love with the handsome piano player. Mary Ellen was already married at the time with a young son, but found she couldn't resist the charms of the dangerous-looking young man. The two would secretly meet for long walks on the beach and then lovemaking in the Marine View Hotel next to Frank's Place.

No one is sure exactly how long the torrid affair lasted, but it ended on a cold November night on the Bayshore Highway. It is believed that Mary Ellen was on her way to meet her lover and was killed when her car skidded off the highway and tumbled end over end. She was wearing a blue dress at the time of the accident, which gives her the name we know her by today.

Another ending to this story has it that Mary Ellen's husband found out about the romance and was determined to end it one way or another. It is said that the husband lay in wait along the beach in hiding and when the couple walked by attacked the piano player with a knife. He was stabbed several times, but would survive his wounds; Mary Ellen was not that lucky. Caught up in his anger and embarrassment, he also lunged for his wife and stabbed her before he fully realized what he was doing and she died there on the beach.

Another twist to this story is the possibility that while the piano player — some say his name was John Contina — was having the affair with Mary Ellen, he was also seeing another woman by the name of Anna Philbrick. Mary Ellen was never aware of this before she died; Anna, however, discovered Mary Ellen and was so distraught…she flung herself off the cliffs near the speakeasy. John, it would seem, was what we would call a player today. It is said that his headless body washed up on shore below Frank's Place a short time after Anna and Mary Ellen's deaths. Could it be that a jealous husband or lover finally caught up with him?

The most famous sighting of the Blue Lady occurred in 1978 when two police officers were traveling home from the Moss Beach Distillery and somehow ended up spinning into a ditch. They were both transported to the hospital for observation, but were concerned that no one seemed to know what happened to the beautiful lady in the blue dress who had been at the accident scene. Over the years the Blue Lady has been spotted along the stretch of highway where it is believed she died.

Many believe this spirit is looking for her piano player and that is why she haunts the Distillery. She has been known to stand on the cliffs, looking out at the ocean, and has on more than one occasion warned children who stray too close to the edge away. Children have also reported seeing her in darkened rooms of the restaurant, as well as many manifestations in the men's bathroom; she will always disappear when an adult arrives.

Since the Moss Beach Distillery has been open, reports of strange happenings have been claimed. Computerized dating systems have been changed to reflect the year 1927; this is the year that Frank's Place originally opened. What is so strange about this is that it repeatedly changed to this year while an employee was inputting the day's receipts and no matter how many times she changed the date it would always revert back to 1927.

Chairs will rearrange themselves in the dining rooms and the sound of high-heeled shoes will be heard walking around in an otherwise empty room. Cases of wine will mysteriously stack themselves against doors in locked rooms and the sound of a woman's voice will be heard, but when an employee goes to investigate there is no one there. People have even seen objects float around the room and then gently place themselves back onto the counter or bar.

Guests dining at the restaurant have, on many occasions, reported light pinches on their necks, taps on their shoulders, their hair tugged, and even hearing their names called in a whispered voice. Women have lost earrings — but only one — in mysterious ways, only to have them and others reappear weeks later stacked on the bar.

One of the reports that has made it into the news and even onto paranormal reality shows is that of the Tiffany lamps that hang over the bar. In times past, people have reported seeing these lamps swing of their own accord, despite never having been touched. Unfortunately, this is something we may never be able to see again, as the current owners of the Distillery have installed "special effects" that now cause the fixtures to sway using electric motors. This high-tech gadget has regrettably caused a lot of people in the paranormal field — as well as others — to doubt the validity of any of the past reports. The owner swears that this computerized effect is solely for the entertainment of the guests and in no way have they tampered with anything else in the way of its haunting activity. You will need to be the judge, but reports were coming from the building long before the reports of this so-called fraud.

There seems to be information of at least three spirits haunting the Moss Beach Distillery. One is believed to be the Blue Lady of course, but her adulterous lover has also been seen on rare occasions and people have even smelled the man's cologne. The third spirit appears to be the man's other lover, Anna Philbrick. All anyone knows about this other entity is that she has been seen at rare times and seems to be draped in seaweed.

When Planet Paranormal investigated the Moss Beach Distillery, we caught no audio or visual evidence. We did notice the swaying bar lamps and were surprised to see an outcropping of rock on the cliffs outside the restaurant that bore an uncanny resemblance to a woman standing on the precipice. This does not mean, however, that the tales are those of the unobservant. There may be some of those, but for me there are too many stories to dismiss them out of hand. It is because of all of the independent sightings and reports that we consider Moss Beach Distillery to have light to moderate paranormal activity.

I highly recommend this upscale piece of California history. They have a diverse menu and seafood lovers will be quite pleased. And the selection of farmhouse favorites will surprise those who prefer the turf rather than the surf. The staff is friendly and attentive and who knows, maybe a pretty young lady clad in a blue dress who seems a bit sad but has a mischievous spirit can serve you.

140 Beach Way
Moss Beach, CA 94038
650-728-5595
mossbeachdistillery.com/
index.html

Visitor's Information
Hours: Monday-Thursday, noon to 8:30 p.m.;
Friday and Saturday, noon to 9 p.m.; and Sundays,
11 a.m. to 8:30 p.m.

Frank's Place is gone and the speakeasy is closed, but today the Moss Beach Distillery is one of the best restaurants on the central coast of California. Their specialty is seafood (their clam chowder is one of the best), but they also have a fine selection of steaks, chicken, and sandwiches. They have a wonderful Sunday brunch and on occasion host a Murder Mystery dinner. Prices range from $15–$34 for entrées and $15–$26 for their signature sandwiches. They have a bar menu, a kids menu, a dessert menu, and even cater to those of us who love dogs with their own dog-friendly patio and dog menu. They have special lodging and dinner packages available as well. Reservations recommended.

Silver City, a Kern River Valley must see.

Silver City Ghost Town

Silver City Ghost Town may not be a real ghost town in the actual sense of the word, but it is an historic piece, or pieces rather, of the entire Kern River Valley. This conglomeration of odd buildings is placed in an almost haphazard manner, yet is still able to project the importance each site has had in the development of the area. J. Paul Corlew is the current owner; he purchased the property in 1988 and has led Silver City into a new, better-known renaissance that promises to keep this historic gem going well into the future. Of course, the spirits that dwell there may say that it is they who have brought the town to its new popularity.

Silver City's inception came when Dave and Arvilla Mills had the idea to start a farm-style amusement park, akin to Knott's Berry farm, so between 1968 and 1972 they began importing buildings from other towns within the Kern Valley, such as Claraville, Keysville, Old Isabella, Whiskey Flats, South Fork, Miracle, and other gold and silver rush towns of the area. Most, if not all, of these towns have disappeared; their remaining buildings having succumbed to the ravages of time and the elements, some to relic hunters, and others to just plain thievery. The fact that the Mills saved as many structures as they did is a testament to their desire to save history itself.

The Mills's dream of an amusement park never materialized due to local politics, but that didn't stop them from opening an attraction unlike any other in the area. Silver City Ghost Town opened in 1968 and had great success, attracting the thousands of drivers that passed by on old Route 178. In the first three years, using signs not only in front of the town, but also along the roadway itself, Silver City pulled in a million visitors. This golden age for the town would not last, however; plans had already been drawn up to widen and straighten Route 178, but the new stretch of road would completely bypass Bodfish and once the new road opened, Silver City, almost overnight, lost its visitors and shuttered its gates. After three years of hard work, this town of historic buildings sat behind a 10-foot fence and was forgotten by all.

For seventeen years, Silver City sat vacant and forlorn. Many of the local citizenry thought the old town had been torn down, but it still remained, withering in the cold winter storms and the dry summer heat. In 1988, J. Paul Corlew purchased the house and adjoining property from the Mills and two years later bought the remainder of the land, which included Silver City. After some hurried but careful restoration on the more dilapidated structures, Corlew reopened the ghost town to the public on Memorial Day Weekend, 1992.

Since that day, Corlew has been lovingly restoring the structures within the town and has opened a unique antique shop out front for his guests to browse, with all the proceeds going toward the restoration. It is Corlew's dream to have his Silver City become not only an attraction, but a source of education about the history of the Kern River Valley as well.

Each building within Silver City tells its own story, has its own imprint, and has its own tale to tell. From the jail, which housed one of the valley's most notorious outlaws, to the church that served the people of Hot Springs for years, this "ghost town" is history itself.

Old Isabella Jail

Built around 1880 in the town of Isabella (which is now under the lake), this jail housed one of the most notorious gunfighters of the area: Newt Walker. The jail itself is a small, two-room affair, which, at the time it was used, had no windows — not even on the door — and may have been crowded with up to twenty prisoners at one time. This lack of windows caused the inside of the cells to be totally dark when shuttered, making the inmates unable to even see their hands in front of their faces, and may well be the cause of one of the most tragic events to take place in this tiny building.

In 1905, it is said that an American Native who had been incarcerated started a fire inside the jail. The reason he started this fire is unknown, although some say the man was trying to stay warm; others say he set the fire against the door as a means of escape. Whichever explanation is correct, what we do know is that the man asphyxiated from the smoke and fumes. With no one to control the fire, the door began to burn and then the rest of the structure ignited. Upon entering the building, the townsfolk found the dead man curled up against the near wall as if he were sleeping.

The "Hanging" tree in the center of town.

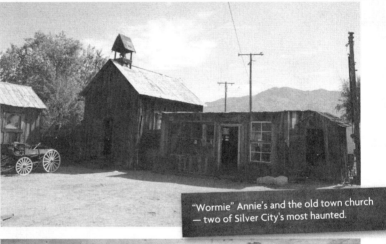

"Wormie" Annie's and the old town church — two of Silver City's most haunted.

Inside "Wormie" Annie's...what do you see in the mirror?

Perhaps the most famous of all tales centered on Kern Valley is that of Newton "Newt" Walker. As gunfighters were concerned, he was an unknown; Billy The Kid, Doc Holliday, and Wyatt Earp were all fast draws in history, but Newt may have been faster still. It is a twisted tale of families feuding over a mining claim that draws Newt into the story, and although he may not have been personally involved, Newt was pulled in nonetheless.

In 1905, Newt, having been implicated years earlier in the killing of Fletcher Burton, was in the town of Havilah with his father when David Burton, Fletcher's brother, and George Bagsby, who some claim was a hired gun, approached them on the street. Bagsby and Burton tried to provoke the younger Walker, but were unsuccessful and the Walkers turned to leave. The taunting continued as they walked away, but Walker still wouldn't respond. Bagsby then shouted, "We want you!", and reached for his pistol. Walker turned, saw the men reaching for weapons, and drew his own, putting two bullets into Bagsby, two into Burton, and then two more into the hired gun for good measure — six bullets were fired by Walker before Bagsby could even pull his weapon free. It was later discovered that Burton was unarmed; although witnesses say he had a gun earlier in the day, Walker was charged with murder.

During Walker's murder trial, the prosecution said it was physically impossible for a man to draw his gun while turning around to face his opponents and place six rounds into them before either could even pull his pistol. The defense countered by asking the judge to allow Walker to demonstrate this feat in the courtroom, which the judge granted. With two stand-ins for the dead men, Walker was given his unloaded .38 and in front of the jury and all present in the courtroom repeated his achievement and was subsequently released from all charges with the jury stating that the shooting was obviously a case of self-defense. This remarkable display of gunmanship is still a tale told in the Kern River Valley today.

Old Hot Springs Baptist Church

This church was brought to Silver City in the late 1960s. It was once the centerpiece of and social hub for the folks of Hot Springs. It was used as a meeting hall, town seat, and, of course, services every Sunday morning. Although Baptist in denomination, no one was ever turned away and any faith was welcome to worship within its walls. This structure was the only church in the town and oversaw all the weddings and funerary services that took place within Hot Springs from the time it was built until the town was deserted some time in the 1960s.

"Wormie Annie" Sullivan's Boathouse

Annie Sullivan is the original owner of the land that Silver City now sits on. Her house (which is still occupied) is behind the ghost town's walls; however, it is visible from the church and is almost close enough to touch. Sullivan got her unusual nickname because one of her many ventures was that of raising earthworms in a building she called her "boathouse." This tiny structure sits in its original location and is now sandwiched between the church building and the Apalatea/Burlando house. Wormie was an irascible character prone to over drinking and what some would deem odd behavior. She would spend countless nights holed up in her boathouse drinking and tending to her worms.

Apalatea/Burlando House

This home is believed to be the oldest structure in the Kern Valley. Built by Francisco Apalatea (pronounced Ah paul ah tay), who, over the years, raised thirteen children (some count it as high as 17) with three different wives in this not-very-large structure. The home was taken over by the Burlando family after marriage to one of the Apalatea daughters and became part of the Burlando ranch, which at the time was the largest ranch in the Kern River Valley. The house was slated for destruction when it was brought to Silver City and now serves as one of the centerpieces of the museum.

There are many other structures within the Silver City complex and each one has a story to tell. The old post office and general store come from the town of Claraville originally, but were moved in the 1950s to the town of Miracle, where they stayed until being moved to Silver City in the late 1960s. The bunkhouse (which is currently undergoing restoration) hails from South Fork, but was originally part of the Peterson Ranch and was built around 1880 as sleeping quarters for Nils Peterson's farm hands.

~~~~~

So much is not known and so much could be learned if these historic walls could talk. What is known, however, is that not all of these buildings arrived at Silver City unoccupied; in fact, many of their long-dead residents seem to have moved to the ghost town along with their homes.

Inside the most haunted place in town — the Apalatea/Burlando House.

Main Street, Silver City.

The original Silver City sign still stands out front.

I was up in the Kernville area with some friends for a weekend rafting trip and we had arrived on Saturday, which was the day before our trip down the Kern River. We were looking for something to do in the evening and the clerk at the motel we were staying at suggested a place called Silver City Ghost Town, which was owned by a friend of his and was only a couple miles away. He told us what the place was all about and it sounded sort of cool, so we decided to give the place a try.

The clerk was right about it being really close to where we were staying, as it only took us about ten minutes to find the place. The first thing we noticed when we got out of the car was that the front looked old…it looked like it was a part of an actual ghost town even though we knew it wasn't. We looked for the entrance, but found the owner of the place in a shop that was filled with some of the oldest and neatest stuff I had ever seen. We paid the small entrance fee, but decided to browse the "relic" store, as I call it, first.

After we had our fill of the shop, we headed into the town proper, where a very friendly cat greeted us. The owner, who had followed us in, explained that the cat, Izzy, was the real owner of Silver City. He then went on to point out some of the buildings — the ones with the most ghost activity — and told us to keep our eyes and ears open. He then left us to explore the town on our own.

There were only one or two people in the town at the same time as us, so we started away from them and checked out the largest building in the town. This place was set up like a bar; however, the owner had told us it was a house, so we were a bit confused. We thought it was kind of cool, though, with the dummies set up as if drinking and playing cards. I looked over at my friend, Jerry, and he had this odd look on his face. I asked him if he felt okay and he just laughed and said, "Yeah, it was weird…I thought for a second that Indian dummy's head moved." We both got a laugh out of that and moved on to look at some of the other houses in the place.

We wandered around for another half-an-hour and by then it was getting dark, so we thought we would find a place to eat, but Jerry wanted to go back to the bar building to have another look at the Indian sitting at the poker table. We headed back over there and just as we looked in I thought I saw the dummy's head turn from looking at the door to facing the wall again. I figured it was the same optical illusion that Jerry had seen, but it was still sort of an odd thing to imagine. Jerry and I both got another laugh out of that until we looked back in the building and noticed that the Indian was now looking directly at us. We hadn't seen the head move, but we both knew it had been looking in the direction of the wall when we had walked up. That was enough for both of us — we headed straight for the exit.

~ Richey Williams

Paranormal Activity

Silver City Ghost Town has been featured in numerous television shows, not only for its historic content, but also for its ghostly happenings. The Apalatea/Burlando house, for example, has, in fact, been designated as the sixth most active home in America for poltergeist activity, just behind the Whaley and Winchester homes. Some of the most incredible claims have come from this remote slice of the Kern Valley.

One Halloween night, while a group of children and their parents were gathered in the Apalatea house, bottles began to float off the shelves, shot glasses moved as if people were drinking at the bar, and one of the mannequins sitting in the rocking chair raised its arm as if waving to the assembled guests. The life-size doll was not designed to move, so it is still unclear how this was accomplished, even if the spirits had moved the dummy. At the same time that things began to move through the air, the guests began to see figures materialize out of thin air and walk from one end of the structure, past the astonished living, and pass through the opposite wall. Owner J. Paul Curlew was giving one of his "lantern light" tours at the time in another part of the town when he heard all the commotion coming from the Apalatea house. He left his group and went to see what was wrong. When he arrived, many of his guests began asking him how he did the special effects and that they were the best they had ever seen. Confused, he tried explaining that there were no special effects, which caused almost all of the parents to rush their children from Silver City as fast as possible. One of the spirits that reportedly haunts the Apalatea/Burlando house is Francisco's third wife Mattie — she is believed to be the spirit that rocks in the rocking chair that many people have seen moving of its own accord.

Over the years, many more reports have come from this structure, mainly the sounds of gaiety and laughter, as if someone is throwing a party. One of the overnight guards heard what he assumed were trespassers carrying on quite loudly in the Apalatea/Burlando house, so he gathered up his retired police dog and headed over to where he heard all the noise. Once he got to the steps of the house and started up them, all of the noise ceased, and when he looked into the open building, he found it was empty. Confused, he turned to his K9 partner, but discovered that the animal was nowhere to be found. It took the guard a few hours of searching, but he finally found the animal cowering under one of the porches of a building furthest from the Apalatea house that the dog could find. The dog would never go near the house again after that night.

The jail is another area where there are numerous reports of paranormal activity. This jail was a cramped, claustrophobic place to be incarcerated and there is at least one known tragic death associated with the building. In the early 1900s, an inmate was found dead from starting a fire in the small cell. Over the years, many children have told their parents that they have seen a man sleeping against the near wall and to be quiet so as not to wake him. When the parents look, there is no one there. The area where the children point is right where the dead inmate was found.

Women seem to be a favorite target of whomever is haunting the jail because, throughout the years, many females have reported their hair being tugged and shoulders gently grabbed, as well as hearing whispered words. Many have also felt their tush being lightly pinched by unseen hands.

Most visitors who come to Silver City know about the paranormal activity of this ghost town. If they don't, then they come to learn about it quickly. Because of this, Corlew is inundated with pictures of orbs and other phenomena that guests have caught on their cameras. One of these pictures shows a very distinct image of a girl in a period dress lurking just inside the jail doorway behind the photo's subject. This photo has had widespread coverage in both newsprint and television.

The Baptist church has had quite a bit of recorded activity as well. A paranormal investigator was alone in the church doing an EVP session when the batteries on numerous pieces of equipment all went dead at the exact same time while simultaneously catching on video a voice saying, "Stop looking at me." Strange balls of light and other light phenomena have also been caught on film within the church.

Perhaps one of the most unusual places in Silver City is that of "Wormie Annie" Sullivan's boathouse. This small, one-room structure seems to have quite a bit of activity and it is believed that Annie herself may be the most prominent spirit. Many pictures have been taken here, and in more than a few the face of a woman will appear, seemingly staring at the photographer from a pane of glass or occasionally the mirror. The face almost always seems to be slightly smiling, as if saying, "Welcome to my place." Is this Annie attempting to let people know she is happy that there are visitors here?

Another unusual feature of this area is the mirror itself. Many people believe that the mirror is a portal to the other side because of how often whole groups of faces and full figures are seen in photos taken of the mirror. One photograph snapped during a lantern light tour shows what appears to be a large spectral audience listening to Corlew speak while his living tourists pay no attention to the glass. The apparitions range from a man wearing a duster and cowboy hat to a little girl in an 1880s-style dress. In all, there seems to be upwards of fifteen figures in the mirror in any given photo.

Spirits have also been seen and photographed on the streets and boardwalks of the town. Corlew, while getting ready to open in the early '90s, thought he saw his young son heading for the gate and called out to stop him. His son spoke out from behind him, which startled Corlew. When he turned back to the youngster he saw at the gate, the child was nowhere to be found. Photos have been shot out in front of the Bordello building that show a cowboy walking along the walkway; however, the boardwalk is so cluttered with mining artifacts as to make that impossible. Shadow people have been reported to inhabit the old 1880s-era cowboy bunkhouse and EVPs are a very common occurrence within the town.

Planet Paranormal has had the pleasure of being the featured investigative group for the lantern light tours on a few occasions and this author has had the privilege of conducting several solo investigations at Silver City. We have captured several EVPs and I have been a victim of the infamous "vortex" mirror — I have several pictures with unexplained figures and faces within the glass. It is due to this that Planet Paranormal rates Silver City as moderate to high paranormal activity.

Virginia City, Tombstone, Calico, and Bodie — most everyone has heard of these famous Wild West towns, but few know of this gem of a ghost town just a couple hours from Los Angeles. J. Paul Corlew has lovingly taken care of this treasure and as the true gentleman he is, he welcomes all those to his town and treats everyone as honored guests. He loves the history of the Kern River Valley and will not hesitate to answer any questions that come his way, but it is the visitors who have kept Silver City alive these many years and it is hoped that it will survive for many more.

If you are looking for a bit of high mountain adventure, head out to Bodfish and say hello to J. and his extended family, for that is what the residents of Silver City are — family. Even if they have been dead for years, they still seem to enjoy visits from the living in this true ghost town.

SILVER CITY GHOST TOWN

3829 Lake Isabella Boulevard
Bodfish, CA 93205
760-379-5146
ghosttown@verizon.net

Visitor Information

Hours (weather permitting): May 15th through September 14th, open daily from 10 a.m. to 4 p.m. (5 p.m. weekends), and September 15th through May 14th, open weekends only 10 a.m. to 4 p.m. Silver City is open other days by chance (call ahead) and anytime by appointment; open holidays except for Thanksgiving Day, Christmas Day, and New Years Day. Hours subject to change.

Daily admission: $5.50 for adults; $4.50 for kids 6-12; free for children 5 and undere

Paranormal investigations: Prices vary and are by appointment only. Contact J. Paul Corlew.

Evening Lantern Light Tours: April 1st through October 31st. These tours feature active paranormal investigations from some of the best-known groups in America. Cost is $12 for adults and children. (Not recommended for younger children.) Call for exact times and dates, or go to their Facebook page.

Northern California

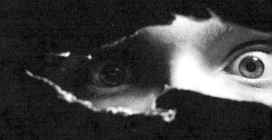

The "Rock" is as imposing today as it was back in the heyday of its use.

Alcatraz Island National Park

It was in the year 1775 that the small island in the North Bay would get its name — that's the year the Spaniards sailed into what is now San Francisco Bay and a young lieutenant spotted an island covered with birds — pelicans to be exact — and so Lt. Juan Manuel de Ayala named the piece of land "Isla de los Alcatraces" (Island of the Pelicans). There are no records indicating if the Spanish actually occupied the island; however, it is known that when they started to construct the mission system in California many of the native Ohlone used the island as a hiding place to escape the Christianity imposed on them. When the Spanish ceded California to Mexico, the island was again forgotten and left to the many birds and wildlife that lived on her and also to the occasional visit by the native population of the area. This all ended in 1848 with the cessation of the Mexican-American War and California, along with Alcatraces, coming under control of the United States. It was around this time that the name of the island was shortened to the Americanized name "Alcatraz." It wasn't long before the military importance of the island as a strategic defensive position for San Francisco Bay was realized and the work of building its fortifications was started. By executive order of President Millard Fillmore, on November 6, 1850, Alcatraz became a U.S. military reservation.

The U.S. Corps of Engineers began its first fortifications in 1853, and the island's first lighthouse was built by the firm Gibbons and Kelly. The lighthouse was lit in 1854, with the large brick citadel, two barracks, and batteries being finished in 1859. Fort Alcatraz was garrisoned on December 20, 1859, and consisted of eighty-five cannon and 130 men. Along with Fort Point and Lime Point, Alcatraz formed a defensive triangle to guard the entrance to San Francisco Bay.

Shortly after the fort was opened, it began taking on military prisoners. These were mostly men who had deserted and were sent to work off their sentence or were put in the hole below what is now called the killing room. This room was the last defense against an attacking force that made it that far up the single road; there they were met by soldiers carrying rifles housed in brick rooms on either side of the pathway. Below one of these rooms is an area where prisoners were housed.

On August 27, 1861, Alcatraz became a military prison and began housing Confederate troops captured during the Civil War. This period also saw the largest military population to live on the island when its force of men grew to 350. As with most prisons at the time, the conditions in the cell house were deplorable, with men sleeping on the stone floor and sickness running rampant; many men could not survive their time in captivity. Because of Alcatraz's importance to the war, it grew substantially during the conflict: a wooden prison was built north of the guard house and later that was built up to become the lower prison. "Bomb-proof" barracks were also added.

After the war, Confederate holdouts, soldiers convicted of heinous crimes, rapists, and murderers were sent to the prison at Alcatraz. Even Native Americans were housed next to the other criminals. The first native to be sent to the island was a man named Paiute Tom, who was transferred from another prison in June 1873; he was shot and killed two days after he arrived by a guard. To this day, the reason for his transfer and the killing have been either lost or covered up. In 1900, the army began sending Philippine prisoners to the island and Alcatraz housed conscientious objectors during World War I. The years 1909 to 1911 saw the army knock down the old citadel and build the prison as we know it today. It was this prison that would later become known as "The Rock."

Alcatraz, or The Rock, was turned over to the Federal Bureau of Prisons in 1934. The timing could not have been better, as the 1930s saw the rise of organized crime in the United States and the need for a maximum-security prison was required to house these violent criminals. The fact that the prison rested on an island surrounded by treacherous ocean currents and the administration took a very strict, hostile approach to the inmates the thirty years that The Rock was open earned it a reputation dreaded by criminals. The inmates at Alcatraz had four rights: food, clothing, shelter, and medical care. Any other comfort or perk was a privilege that had to be earned; these included receiving visits or mail from family, access to the recreation yard, and access to the library or music area. If an inmate could go five years with good behavior and the warden considered them to pose no threat, then they might be transferred to a different prison to finish out their sentence. Conversely, an unruly inmate in another prison could find himself transferred to Alcatraz for bad behavior.

Nighttime on fog-shrouded Alcatraz.

C block and the notorious D block...where one could find themselves in solitary.

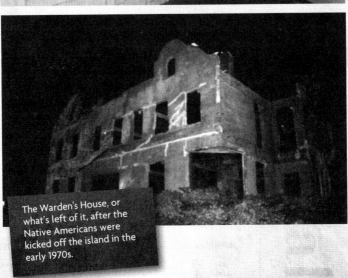

The Warden's House, or what's left of it, after the Native Americans were kicked off the island in the early 1970s.

One of the most famous inmates to be locked up at Alcatraz was Al Capone. Capone had been at the Atlanta Penitentiary and had been quite successful at bribing the guards to the point that anything Al wanted Al got. He even moved his family nearby so he could still run his crime empire through them. When Capone arrived on The Rock, he tried to charm Warden Johnston, but was unable to; all Johnston would say was to give Capone his number — inmate 85 — and directed him to get back in line with the other inmates. For four and a half years, Capone would try to persuade Johnston, but it got him nowhere. Another famous gangster to spend time on the island was "Machine Gun" Kelly, who spent seventeen years at Alcatraz.

Life on The Rock was one of routine: wake up at 6:30 and walk silently to the mess, work the day, march silently back to the mess for dinner, and then walk silently back to your cell. Every half-hour the inmates were counted. The prison had a strict rule of silence that was rigorously enforced. Many inmates found this rule to be the hardest to abide by and many were disciplined and put in solitary confinement for breaking this rule. It is rumored that inmates would actually go insane from the silence.

It is not surprising that one would not want to remain on this island prison. Even though the inmates knew that the sea surrounding Alcatraz was dangerous, there were still fourteen escape attempts while the prison was in operation. The first occurred in 1936 when Joe Bowers was shot by a guard and died. The next year, Theodore Cole and Ralph Roe were swept out to sea, and in 1938, three inmates killed a guard; one of the inmates was killed while the other two were caught. Again and again, this would go on over the years with no success. One of the worst attempts is known as "The Battle of Alcatraz." It happened in May of 1946: six prisoners overpowered the guards, but could not find the keys to the cellblock. Eighteen officers were injured and two killed before the Marines, who were called in, could regain control. Three of the inmates surrendered, but three others who tried to escape through a utility corridor were later found dead, wedged between pipes. Today, one can still see where grenades from the Marines exploded. Perhaps the most famous escape attempt was by Frank Morris and the Anglin brothers. Clint Eastwood starred in the movie *Escape from Alcatraz* that brought the three men notoriety. In June of 1962, the inmates, in an elaborate scheme, managed to elude the guards and get away. Although a body was found several weeks after the escape, the three men are still listed as missing and presumed drowned.

Because the prison was located on an island, which required that all provisions, including water, had to be brought in by boat, the cost of maintaining Alcatraz was much higher than other prisons of similar size. Coupled with the $3-5 million need for restoration and maintenance, it was decided The Rock would close. After twenty-nine years of operation, the federal prison at Alcatraz closed its doors on March 21, 1963. For the next six years, Alcatraz sat empty until a group of Native Americans tried to claim the island as Indian land and a diverse group from many tribes took up illegal residence. The leaders of this group could not maintain control and Alcatraz suffered because of it. Over the next eighteen months, the Warden's house burnt down and then a fire destroyed the lighthouse keeper's home. When the Marshals finally removed the squatters, it was found they had vandalized many of the other buildings and graffiti was everywhere. In 1973, Alcatraz reopened under the umbrella of the Golden Gate National Recreation Area and has become one of the most popular sites in the system. It is so popular that it is recommended that reservations for the tours be made many months in advance.

Paranormal Activity

The first deaths to occur on Alcatraz were in 1857 when two laborers were killed in a landslide, but they were by no means the last. An epidemic some time in the late 1800s caused many deaths and the army was never very conscientious in watching its prisoners; that, coupled with its time as a federal prison for some of the most violent and murderous criminals in the country, and you have a perfect recipe for paranormal stew. Today, the reports of activity are widespread and frequent. The ghost of Al Capone has supposedly been heard playing his banjo in the shower room, where he would practice while the rest of the population was in the recreation yard. In the infirmary ward, employees have told of hearing whispered voices and screams coming from the operating area. The mess hall is also an area where voices are heard, as well as knocks and the sound of utensils. The utility corridor at the end of the cell blocks, where inmates Coy, Hubbard, and Cretzer were riddled with bullets while hiding from the guards after the Battle of Alcatraz, has had reports of unexplained clanging sounds coming from inside, and cell blocks A and B have had reports of crying and moaning emanating from nowhere and everywhere. However, no matter how many reports come from the other areas of the prison, none of them compare with the disturbances associated with Cellblock D.

The D-Block is said to be the most haunted area in all the prison. This area of Alcatraz was by far the worst a prisoner could get. Only one trip to the recreation yard and two showers a week was allowed and all meals were served in the cells, so no contact was permitted with the other inmates. Thirty-eight of the cells were identical to those on the other cellblocks, but four were termed "isolation" — these cells had only one low-wattage light bulb, which was controlled by the guards, and the mattress was only put in the cell at lights out. The door was a solid piece of metal, closing off the occupant from all contact with other souls. These cells were for the inmates who broke the rules. The worst of these cells was 14-D. Located at the very end of the block, it did not even contain a sink or toilet…only a small hole in the floor for the convicts to relieve themselves. No light bulb was issued for light and the prisoner was not allowed clothing while in this cell — the coldest cell on the island. Guards as early as the 1940s would report seeing a figure of a man in 1800s attire walking the hallway next to these cells.

Legend tells of an inmate who was locked in 14-D one night that began yelling that a man was in the cell with him and he was being attacked. The guard, knowing that he was in the room by himself, ignored the prisoner. The man continued to yell for many hours until he grew silent. The next morning, when the guards checked on the convict, they found him dead — the look on his face one of abject terror. The handprints found on his neck indicated murder, and although he was alone in his cell, the autopsy confirmed the death a homicide. Shortly after his death, it was said that he showed up in the morning line-up. As the stunned guards and inmates looked on, he simply vanished. Many believe that the ghostly prisoner that walks the block is the one who murdered the convict in cell 14-D.

To this day, visitors to this cellblock experience eerie feelings walking along the corridors and intense feelings of dread when entering the cells, as well as extreme sudden drops in temperature. It was cell 14-D that started Planet Paranormal's founder, Robert Davis, on his long journey of research into the paranormal. Bob was thirteen years old when his parents took him on a tour of Alcatraz. While in the D-block, the tour guide asked if anyone was brave enough to lock themselves in 14-D. Bob was not a believer at the time and said he would do it. The cell door closed and he was plunged into darkness…immediately he was grabbed on the shoulder and a voice said into his ear, "You're mine." Being only thirteen, his reaction was to be expected and he has been searching for answers ever since.

The laundry room on cellblock C is said to house an unseen presence believed to be Abie Maldowitz, also known as Butcher, who was killed in the laundry room as retaliation for murdering another prisoner. From the show *Sightings*, guards who were interviewed have stated they hear unexplained crashing sounds, running footsteps, screams, moans, metal rattling, feelings of being watched, and cell doors that close on their own. While touring the prison, the late Peter James could hear the voices of men in pain and experienced feelings of fear, pain, and insanity.

Planet Paranormal was lucky enough to have spent the night on Alcatraz, and what we found was one of the most haunted areas we have ever seen. We had been told no one had ever really investigated the lower section on the island, so we decided that would be a good place to start. We were not disappointed. Almost immediately upon entering the killing room, we began hearing voices in the area. Thinking it was another group, we began searching for their whereabouts, but no one could be found. We did catch two Class A EVPs in the area; one was of a woman who seemed very surprised that we were talking to her/them. In the mess hall, we could hear knocking and banging in the kitchen area, which was inaccessible, as if some one was preparing a meal. At one point, it looked as though someone quickly stepped between rooms in the isolated back kitchen. When passing by the lighthouse keeper's house, two of our members twice thought they could see someone looking back at us. The infirmary was open to us and it was this area that by far turned in the most activity. We received EVPs in just about every room we entered; in the isolation ward, one of our members was all but pushed from the chair he was sitting in while at the same time we picked up an audible voice telling us to "get out." Weird feelings and cold spots were constant companions as we self-guided ourselves on a tour of the most haunted island in America. We consider Alcatraz to have high to extremely high paranormal activity.

Today, Alcatraz is a bird sanctuary and recreation area; however, even today visitors experience cold spots, chills, and feelings of unease. These are grim reminders of a time the island was used as a place of punishment and, for some, torture for men who could not abide by the law, even while in prison. So when you visit, keep in mind that some of the people you see may not be who you think they are — they just may be tour guides from another era showing you *their* big house.

I was taking a night tour of Alcatraz Island one night in July and had just finished the audio tour part and was wandering around the shower area taking pictures. I had been in the prison once or twice during the day and found the night tour to be much more entertaining; the prison was the same, but the atmosphere was definitely different. During the day, the dim lighting is offset by the sunlight, so that even in the darkest areas of the prison there is still light enough to see all the nooks and crannies; at night, all of these places are covered in shadow and the cold of the cement building is felt down to the bone.

Like I said, I was taking pictures of the area around the shower, which consisted of the barber shop, prison laundry storage, uniform storage, and, of course, shower stalls. I had heard the stories about how people have heard the sound of violin music coming from this area and that it was supposed to be Al Capone who was playing, so I was concentrating on staring at the shower section in the hope I would hear the music. What I heard was anything but that. As I concentrated on the shower, a scream came from the barbershop area — this was not a quiet, whispered scream, but a loud wailing that sounded as if someone was being killed. I turned toward the sound, but the shop was empty and there was no other sound coming from the area. I waited for a couple minutes, but nothing else happened. To this day, I have no idea what I heard or why I heard it, but it is something I will remember till the day I die.

~ Jason Bigmon

ALCATRAZ ISLAND NATIONAL PARK

Fort Mason, Bldg. 201
San Francisco, CA 94123
Visitor Info: 415-561-4900
Reservations: 415-705-5555

The "cowpokes saloon" in Banta, California.

Banta Inn

The town of Banta, in Northern California, is located between the cities of Tracy and Stockton and was named after Henry Banta, who settled there in the 1800s. It was a major interchange point for the Central Pacific and Southern Pacific railroads and was located along the route of the transcontinental railroad from Sacramento to the San Francisco bay area by way of the Altamont pass before the Central Pacific bought the route of the California Pacific. Due to its location, the tired traveler visited there often.

In 1879, Frank Gallegos, whom local lore says was at one time a member of outlaw Joaquin Murrieta's band, built a two-story sporting house and saloon. Since the upper floors had rooms, it was given the title of an inn and it briefly spent time as a stage stop. However, the rooms had been added for another purpose — soon after opening, the Banta Inn became a house of ill repute. It remained this way for quite some time; then, in 1937, most of the building was destroyed in a fire. Tragically, a young mother and her daughter were killed in the blaze while sleeping in one of the second-floor rooms. Very quickly, the inn was rebuilt to its current status as a single-story structure. Many of the original timbers were used during the new construction. Banta was also a popular stop along the famous Lincoln Highway, which ran from New York City to San Francisco; although not as well known as Route 66, it was still an important part of the history of our car culture.

In the 1960s, the Banta Inn was still owned by Frank Gallegos's youngest daughter, Jenny, by now Jenny Gukan. Jenny's husband, Tony, spent much of his time at the Banta, as cook, houseboy, or anything else needed to keep the place running. However, his notoriety to the locals came as the Banta Inn's bartender. Tony had a few noticeable habits, such as playing cards alone in the corner, cards held in both hands playing poker against himself. Another oddity was keeping the cash drawer open behind the bar when he worked, and he would also, subconsciously, stack the coins he received into nice, neat, tidy rows in the same money drawer he left open. In 1968, while behind the bar, Tony suffered a major heart attack, and even though rescue was just across the street, it was still too far away to save Tony. He died behind the bar doing what he loved in the place he called home.

The Gukan family owned the Banta Inn until 1981 when a new proprietor took the reins. The new owners were true to the establishment and changed very little. Today, even though it has changed hands once again, it is still the same, as one would expect from, as it says over the door, "A cowpokes saloon."

Paranormal Activity

The Banta Inn has a long history of paranormal activity and has been featured on the shows *Unsolved Mysteries*, *Sightings*, and, with Lloyd Auerbach, *Hard Copy*. Some of the activity reported include beer bottles being moved from tables, potatoes popping out of the oven, people's hair being tugged, the voice of a little girl being heard, a woman outside on the patio being seen (someone who may have been murdered in the early 1900s), the sound of a baby crying, and even the occasional, but rare, apparition. Perhaps the most famous occurrence is that of coins mysteriously stacking themselves on the bar. Many believe this is indeed Tony Gukan, letting people know he is still looking out for the place he cared for in life.

The current owner of the Banta Inn is one of the nicest people we have met and has given the Planet Paranormal team full access both times we have been there to investigate, and the team would like to thank him for his trust and support. During both these times, we have had a few personal experiences, such as a DVR camera that we had taped down being moved off the bar. Two of our team members were sitting at the bar doing EVP work when they heard the sound of papers rustling, which seemed to be the work schedule papers moving on the wall in the kitchen area. Also from the kitchen, the entire team heard the very loud noise of what sounded like many beans falling and scattering across the floor, yet there was nothing amiss when we went to check what had fallen. Quite a few shadows were seen moving around the bar area when the team was in the dining room and at one time a member had to go out in front to find out who was moving around, only to find no one there. We did catch a couple of EVPs of a girl saying "Lie down." At this same time, our founder's hair stood up as if by an electric charge and we caught another EVP that is definitely a female's voice, but the words are unintelligible.

We consider the Banta to have light to medium paranormal activity, but this piece of history 90 minutes from Oakland is a must for the food and the great staff. And who knows, maybe Tony will stack some change for you and let you know he still cares for the customers in death as he used to in life.

On Friday nights, see the Banta Inn rock with live music, dancing, and, of course, spirits.

Money, beer, and football — why would the spirits ever think of leaving home?

The rustic decor of the Banta Inn welcomes both the living and the dead.

My husband and I just love the Banta Inn. The atmosphere is a little blue collar, but that just adds to the charm of the place and has always made us feel relaxed and comfortable there. We had always known the place was supposedly haunted from seeing it on TV, both local and national shows, and we have talked to the people working there about it many times. They have always assured us that it is definitely haunted, as they have all personally had "things" happen to them. We had always just smiled and thought what a wonderful sales tool they had created.

On a recent Friday night we had decided to go to the Banta because we were both craving one of their famous steaks. It was a warm night, so we decided to sit out on the back patio and listen to the band they had playing. It was a local "tribute" band and they were pretty good. We ordered a couple beers and sat listening while we waited for our dinner to arrive. The place was sorta crowded, being early on a Friday night, and there were only one or two families eating, but they were in the main dining room. I did notice, however, that there was a young girl standing in front of the small low stage. She couldn't have been more than 13 years old and I remember thinking that her mother or father was being inattentive by allowing her to be outside by herself that close to the stage, but figured since it was a closed patio I would just ignore her as best I could and hope she wouldn't go deaf.

As I was eating my dinner, I would glance over now and then and check to see if the girl was still staring at the band and to make sure she was still safe. I happened to look down at my watch and realized that it had been quite awhile since we had arrived and that the families with children had already been eating by the time we got to the restaurant. I thought it was kind of odd that people with children should linger at a place like this and my mind began to worry that something might be wrong. I told my husband that I was going to go inside for a minute to see if I could find the parents of the little girl, but he just stared at me with a confused look. I got up from the table, gave my husband a playful swat for the vacant look on his face, and went inside. I looked around for a couple minutes, but could not locate anyone with a family or anyone who looked as if they were looking for a little girl, so I went and asked the waitress if anybody asked about their child being missing; she told me that no one had a lost child and all of the families had left over half an hour earlier.

I was a bit confused as I walked back to our table, but figured maybe the girl was with someone in the band, which would make sense as to why she was standing so close to the stage. I looked over to where the little girl had been standing, but she was no longer standing where she had been. I scanned the area, but could not find her anywhere. I know she hadn't gone inside because there was only one door back into the Inn and I would have noticed her enter. I asked my husband if he had seen where she had gotten off to and he asked me who. I told him the little girl I asked him to watch and he said, "What girl, I didn't know who you meant when you said that the first time?" I told him the girl that was standing next to the stage listening to the band; he said that he had been watching the band play the whole time we had been outside and that he never saw a girl standing by the stage and he would have noticed. Confused, I waited until the band had stopped playing and asked them about her, but they said no little girl was with them and none of them remembered seeing her while they played. It seems no one I asked had seen this child either. I mentioned it to our waitress who just shrugged her shoulders and smiled. I am either crazy or I saw this girl when no one else had. I can't explain it, but I know I am NOT crazy.

~ Marcy

BANTA INN

22563 So. 7th Street
Banta, CA 95304
209-835-1311
www.bantainn.net

Visitor Information

Today the Banta Inn is run as a family restaurant and bar. They have a large menu, but specialize in big juicy burgers and tender, hand-cut, cooked to order steaks. They also serve pasta and offer daily specials including prime rib.

A country breakfast is served beginning at 8 a.m.

Monday & Tuesday kids 10 and under eat free.

On Sunday night they have All You Can Eat spaghetti, garlic bread, and salad from 4 to 8 p.m.

Friday's specials are Clam chowder and Prime Rib.

Live music Friday's 8 to 10 p.m. and karaoke Wednesdays from 8 p.m. to 12 a.m.

Banquet room and Patio with a stage for your party planning and full catering service are available.

The ghost town of Bodie, a town held in a state of "arrested decay."

Bodie State Park

"Goodbye God, we are going to Bodie!"
"The worst climate out of doors one can imagine."
"A sea of sin, lashed by the tempest of lust and passion!"
"The bad man of Bodie."

These are just some of the things said about the gold rush boomtown in California called Bodie.

Now a ghost town persevered "in a state of arrested decay" by the State parks service, Bodie at one time was said to be second only to San Francisco in size (there is some dispute of this claim), but had a reputation to match or exceed that of Dodge City and Deadwood in lawlessness and violence. It was said that a shooting occurred everyday and that stage holdups and street fights were common.

Bodie had its start in 1858 when four prospectors, drawn by the stories of gold, traveled through a small valley by Mono Lake. One of these fortune seekers was W. S. Bodey. His first name has a bit of mystery surrounding it, as a woman claiming to be his widow has identified him as William, Waterman, or Wakeman. What is known, however, is that he died while returning to his diggings when a violent snowstorm hit the area and never had a chance to spend his gold or see the town that would bear his name. The spelling of Bodie comes from a sign painter who, not liking the original spelling of Bodey, decided to change it to its current form, thinking it looked better and could not be as easily mispronounced. The townsfolk agreed and the place would forever more be known as "Bodie."

Bodey's partner, "Little Black" Taylor, laid the Montauk claim directly over the spot W. S. had found the placer ground. As this discovery took place at the same time as the discovery of silver in nearby Aurora, Nevada, and the Comstock Lode at Virginia City, interest in Bodie remained lackluster and by 1868 only two companies had mills at Bodie and they were failing. Harsh terrain and weather, coupled with the low ore output, caused Bodie to go unnoticed and virtually unmined for the next seven years...until 1875, when the Bunker Hill mine caved in and exposed a large ore vein that brought immediate attention to the destitute town.

By 1877, the town had grown to a population of about 4,000 people and brought Bodie to the attention of investors from the Bay area. These investors bought the Bunker Hill claim for $67,500; they changed the name and incorporated the mine as the Standard Company in April of that year. In that year alone the Standard Company produced $784,523 in gold and silver ore, which made the stockholders quite happy and wealthy. The Standard's good fortune allowed them to build a new, larger stamp mill.

The Standard strike and another at the Bodie Mine in 1878 attracted even more people to the area, and by 1879, Bodie had a population of between 5,000 and 7,000 people and approximately 2,000 buildings. Investors from as far away as New York poured money into the area and by the end of the year twenty-two mines using the latest and most expensive equipment had sprung up.

As miners and merchants began arriving to the town, so did the human element of greed. This, along with the rough conditions of the area, gave rise to people living "for the moment." The winter of 1878-79 was a particularly harsh one and saw hundreds of deaths from exposure and many more from illness and disease. Mine accidents were common and took their toll on the people of Bodie as well. Even through all the hardship the town still grew.

A reporter for the *Daily Bodie Standard* wrote: "The stages come in loaded with passengers and go out loaded with bullion." By 1880, Bodie had 11,000 residents, thirty mines, sixty-five saloons, three newspapers, a post office, gambling halls, numerous brothels, a china town replete with opium dens, three breweries, even its own brass band — but not a single church. Those weren't built until 1882, and then only two. The Chinese were used as household servants and cheap manual labor. Because the surrounding area had no trees, wood was at a premium and the Chinese used to ship it in by the wagonload. When the Bodie & Benton Railroad was complete, it began bringing wood to the town at a rate of 100,000 cords a year. The rail company hired inexpensive Chinese labor that angered the many unemployed miners in the area.

In the late 1880s, it became clear that the mother lode that everyone assumed would be found at Bodie did not exist. Many mines that appeared promising in the early days of the boom were abandoned while others were mined only on a part-time basis due to lack of ore rock. Facing another harsh winter with no hope for employment, as well as word of rich strikes in Montana and Arizona, men and families began to leave *en masse*. The Standard Company and a few others with financial backing continued to mine and make a profit, but the smaller mines started

Bodie was abandoned slowly, yet even today one can almost feel the people still lingering.

Even the most personal things were left to the high desert wind.

The town refuses to die and the determination of its people seems to be imbued into the remaining buildings.

to fail, as the ore veins grew deeper and deeper into the ground. By 1883, only eight hundred people remained in the town, and then in 1892 a fire broke out and destroyed a large portion of the town, further reducing the population.

The Standard continued mining and reached a depth of 1,200 feet, with the Lent reaching that same level a few years later. This did nothing to stop the decline in ore rock and the Standard Company was forced to find ways to reduce costs to stay solvent. In 1893, they built what would become the country's first long-distance electrical transmission plant above the town of Bridgeport. This hydroelectric plant was deemed a joke by the townsfolk and they all gathered to laugh at the folly of the idea as the switch was thrown for the first time. It took several minutes for the lights to flicker to life, but when the laughter died the Standard had its own, cheaper source of electricity. The Bodie Mining Company sold out to the Standard in 1896, which was not a good buy for the company and they were forced to sell out in 1913.

James S. Cain purchased the Standard mine in 1914, along with everything else he could get his hands on. In 1915, the mines put out more than $100,000 in profit. Unfortunately, it was a case of "too little, too late" to stop the town's decline. The Standard closed again in 1917, running for six years after the power plant was destroyed by an avalanche in 1911. In 1915, the Mono Lake Railway & Lumber Company (formerly the Bodie & Benton Railway) was closed, its rails sold as scrap and its ties abandoned, as auto travel began to captivate the country. Bodie was already being called a ghost town, and by 1920, the census had its population at 120.

The town continued to have permanent residents, even though the decline was in full swing. A well-financed mining company reopened the Red Cloud mine briefly, but suffered heavy losses and closed down after only two years; then, in 1932, the story goes that "Bodie Bill," an upset toddler, set fire to his house over not having a birthday cake and the resulting conflagration destroyed 95% of the remaining town.

The last major operation to take place in Bodie was the Roseklip. Machinery was brought in to treat the rock discarded and piled at the mine entrances. However, instead of rebuilding the town, employees found lodging in the remaining buildings that had survived the fire. After only a six-year run, though, World War II started and the federal government ordered all mines to stop. The Lucky Boy, the last operating mine, shut down and mining operations ceased for good. The last residents moved out and Bodie became an actual ghost town.

The Cain family, fearing vandals, hired caretakers to oversee and maintain the town's structures until they finally deeded the land to the State of California. In 1961, the town was listed as a national historic landmark; in 1962, the surviving structures were taken over by the Department of Parks and Recreation and two years later, the town was dedicated as Bodie State Historic Park by the California Park Commission.

Over the years Bodie's mines produced an estimated $34 million worth of gold. The Standard, of all the mines in and around Bodie, accounted for $18 million in gold and silver and paid out just over $5 million in dividends to its stockholders in its thirty-seven years of operation.

I am a retired ranger for the California Park service and worked at Bodie back in the early 1970s. When I saw your request, I thought that this would be a great time for me to get something off my chest that had been bothering me for many years. As a park services ranger for the State of California, I was not allowed to talk about any strange or odd occurrences that took place at the park, but now that I am coming to the end of the line as it were of my life, I feel that I should let people know about the ghost town.

As I said, I have been retired for many years, but I will always remember the winter of [omitted for added privacy]. I was scheduled for caretaker duty over the winter and was staying at the old "Cain" house. This is one of the structures at the park that has been upgraded as a house for rangers that "live" on the site and there is always one or two of us there, especially during the long winter days while the park is closed to visitors. This year it was myself and two other rangers we will call "Bob" and "Sandy."

The first thing that I can remember happening is one day while I was making my rounds around the town I caught what seemed to be the sound of a party. The noise seemed to be coming from where the old Chinese section of town had been located, which was odd due to the fact that there are not really any structures left standing there. I walked toward that area, but the noise stopped before I got near. I continued on, but when I arrived there was no sound other than the wind coming down the pass. This actually happened to myself, Bob, and Sandy a number of times throughout the winter.

Over the months one of us would always come back from doing our duty and relate a tale of food cooking, or the sound of children playing, horses moving down the empty streets, and just the sounds of a town that was still living, but one that we knew was dead. When we would make our rounds in the evening, we would hear the sounds of people enjoying themselves in the bars that were no longer open and even the sounds of gambling and laughter from other structures. On one Sunday morning we even thought we could hear the sound of mass coming from the old church! These were not everyday occurrences; sometimes we would go a week or more without anything strange happening, but it happened enough that we began to understand why the park service might not want us to talk about these things.

All of these events that occurred outside around the town were disturbing, but they were not the only things that were going on. We had quite a few things occur inside the Cain house as well. It started with just some minor things, such as doors we knew to be closed would be wide open upon our return home or the smell of something wonderful cooking in the kitchen…only to find the stove cold and nothing sitting on the counter to eat.

We would be sitting in the small common room chatting about our lives away from town and would start hearing music playing from other rooms within the house…only to find upon investigation that there was only silence. Sandy even thought he had seen someone through one of the windows, but knew that Bob and I were out checking on other areas of the town at the time. When he went in to search, he found that all the doors were locked and there was no one inside. We had heard the tales about this house and town, but until this winter none of us ever really believed them. Now, however, we understood that Bodie was indeed still inhabited by its former residents.

We mentioned all of these occurrences to our superiors, but all they would say was that we were to remember that we were not allowed to tell anybody about anything that happened or we would face discipline up to and including termination. Why the state is so adamant about not telling the truth about Bodie and how many other state parks is something I will never understand, but it is something that I personally believe should be public record and I hope that me telling you about this for your book will be the first step in California being open to its residents. Thank you.

~ Anonymous

Paranormal Activity

Reports of paranormal activity are many and range from phantom smells and cold spots to being touched and even sat upon. One of the more popular stories revolves around the Cain House. The house sits at the corner of Park and Green streets and is said to be haunted by a female Chinese woman who seems to dislike adults, but has a fondness for children. Mr. Cain hired this woman to tend to his house and be a nanny to his children. Although she was good at her job, Jim Cain was forced to fire her over the rumor that she had become his mistress. The woman, in a state of disgrace, was not able to find work after she was let go and eventually committed suicide. Over the years, the building has been used to house families of the park rangers and they have reported doors opening and closing on their own, the face of a Chinese woman appearing at an upstairs window, and music playing in a bedroom that was unoccupied. The most frightening tales, however, have been reports of people sleeping in the house and being awoken by the feeling of someone sitting on them, sometimes to the point of suffocation. One woman even ended up on the floor trying to dislodge whatever was causing the feeling, only to discover that there was nothing there when she finally stood up.

The Mendocini House is another home where reports of spirit activity are common. Mrs. Mendocini herself is believed to be one of the friendly ghosts that inhabit the structure. Being Italian, Mendocini loved to cook and entertain guests. The smell of her cooking has been noticed on many occasions, as well as the sounds of partying. The laughter of children has also been reported outside in the yard.

In the Gregory House, guests have seen an old woman sitting in a rocking chair knitting or have seen the chair seemingly rocking on its own. The Dechambeau House has an old woman who likes to look out at the world from an upstairs window, and at other locations in the town, staff and guests have reported the feeling of being watched from windows of various buildings, being followed down walkways, and seeing objects move while peering into the interiors of many structures.

Even the old cemetery has had its share of reported activity. Around a grave topped by a white marble angel, an entity is said to play with the children visiting Bodie. The grave is that of a three-year-old girl accidentally killed by a blow to the head. She is known as "The Angel of Bodie."

There are no violent or dangerous ghosts in Bodie. However, one of the more frightening is believed to be that of a man named Ed. There were six residences in Bodie in the mid-1940s when Ed, in a drunken rage, shot and killed his wife. The story goes that three of the other men still living in the town formed a small lynch mob and either hanged Ed or beat him to death. Either way, Bodie was down to four living souls. A few months after Ed's murder, his ghost returned and within weeks all three men died under mysterious circumstances. After that, Bodie truly became a ghost town.

Perhaps the most famous paranormal aspect of Bodie would be its curse. Legend has it that anyone removing an item from the town will be cursed with bad luck. This not only includes items stolen from structures and machinery, but pebbles and stones that find their way home with guests. The Rangers keep a book of the items returned each year by people hoping to break the string of catastrophic events that plague their lives after removing Bodie paraphernalia. Letters of apology not only to the park staff, but also the spirits of the town, accompany many of these items as well. Some of these letters are on display in the museum. Some believe the curse is caused by the protective ghosts of Bodie; others say it's a ruse of the Park Rangers to help preserve the historic town.

No EVPs or photographic evidence were captured while investigating Bodie, but that does not mean that the spirits have given up the ghost at the town. Entities are not circus performers acting on cue; however, if you visit the town, you will get the feeling they remain. We consider Bodie to have moderate activity.

Many people are interested in real haunted ghost towns. Bodie may be one of the most famous for its hauntings and is by far the most visited. Each year amateur ghost hunters and paranormal teams flock to the town in hopes of catching evidence of the supernatural and each year these individuals are told to stop and just enjoy the town. TV shows are denied access, and the curious are told by Park Rangers "we are not allowed to talk about that." The head Ranger told the author, "Bodie is a historic ghost town. Not a historic town of ghosts." The State of California has the official position that all Rangers are forbidden to speak about the paranormal or face discipline or termination. This includes all state parks, Alcatraz included, state historic sites, and missions. This does not, however, preclude you from investigating these sites as long as you obey all laws of the park system. Have fun and be aware that you are being watched — not only by the Rangers, but also by the townsfolk who still call Bodie home.

BODIE STATE PARK

P.O. Box 515
Bridgeport, CA 93517
760-647-6445
www.bodie.net
www.parks.ca.gov/default.asp?page_id=509

The Gay Nineties Pizza parlor is a mainstay for not only the people of Pleasanton, but for those that refuse to pass on.

Gay Nineties Pizza Company

Built in 1864 to house the Wells Fargo offices, this building was one of the first commercial structures in the town of Pleasanton. Along with the business office, it also contained a general store and a bar. Local legend has it that the site was used at one time as a stage stop; however, the curator at the Wells Fargo museum in San Francisco says it was never used in that capacity because Pleasanton was too small. The stagecoaches stopped in the town of Dublin instead. After the transcontinental railroad came through in 1869, the building was used as a delivery and receiving station for Wells Fargo. Wells Fargo travelers who were staying in town to conduct their transactions occupied the ten rooms on the upper floor.

During the 1870s, Pleasanton had a growing population of Chinese immigrants who came to the area to work on the railroad system. These men were not looked upon highly by the residents and were discouraged from interacting with the locals. Because of this, it is rumored that a network of tunnels was dug underneath the town that the Chinese would use to travel from one establishment to another in order to avoid contact with hostile residents. It is said that many actually took to living in the tunnels, which collapsed in the 1920s when Main Street was paved.

Not much has changed over the years, but that's just the way the spirits like it.

Where the infamous "Chinese" tunnel entrance was located in the basement of the Gay Nineties Pizza parlor.

Today, in the basement of the Gay Nineties Pizza, the remains of one of these tunnel entrances is said to be boarded up, but still present. Note: There is no physical or photographic evidence to prove that a network of tunnels ever existed. We do know that there was a tunnel built from the jail to the courthouse at 855 Main Street, now the Pleasanton Hotel, to make moving prisoners easier and safer.

From 1901 to 1902, the building housed a saloon called The Club House. In 1903, new owners took over and it became The Blue Goose. It is believed the upper rooms were turned into a brothel when it was The Club House and continued as such until The Blue Goose closed sometime in 1904, when the Lucas Paint Shop began operating at the location. Since then, the building has had many retail establishments, including restaurants, occupying it. The Gay Nineties Pizza Company set up shop in the late 1970s and has established a loyal clientele not only for their superb food, but also for the ghosts that call the restaurant home.

Paranormal Activity

One of the better-known occurrences at the Gay Nineties revolves around the front mirror. Sometime in the 1980s the owner heard a commotion in the dining room. While looking at the mirror, the owner was shocked to see the word "Boo" appear as he watched. He said it was as if someone was drawing it out with a finger. To this day, no matter how many times the mirror is cleaned, the words reappear. Planet Paranormal was witness to this phenomena when we investigated the location.

Another well-known story is that of voices being heard in the basement near where the old tunnel is said to be. These voices are speaking Chinese, which lends credence to the theory that the immigrants lived in or near the tunnels. Coughing and the sounds of gaming, possibly mahjong, are also heard in this area.

Many people have claimed to witness the apparition of a woman, usually in Victorian dress, standing in one of the upper windows. This upper floor was once used as overnight accommodations for weary Wells Fargo employees, as well as a short stint as a brothel. The Victorian dress would seem to predate the brothel era; therefore, we can assume she may be an overnight guest or perhaps a Wells Fargo hostess. Passersby have reported that she stands at the window looking into the night; she will watch for a minute and then vanish.

There is also a story told by the employees about the owner's son. One year at Christmas, he had invited his parents to have dinner at the restaurant for the holiday. They had just sat down to eat when his young son asked him who the lady was and would she be joining them. The owner and his parents turned toward where the boy was pointing and were surprised to see a woman dressed as a dance hall girl looking out the window. As they watched, she faced them, smiled, and then vanished. Quite a few years later, as one of the employees was cleaning up, a picture fell off the wall and broke. Behind the first print was discovered a very old picture of a scantily clad woman in a sexy pose. Could this be the same dance hall girl the owner and his family saw that Christmas day?

Cold spots and odd noises are commonplace, as are phantom footsteps and doors opening and closing on their own. Lights have been known to shut off and then turn themselves back on, and employees and guests alike have reported catching glimpses of things moving out of the corner of their eyes. We consider this site to have mild to moderate activity.

If you are ever in the town of Pleasanton, California, and are in the mood for some truly fine pizza, then a trip to the Gay Nineties Pizza Company is a must. The food is fantastic, the staff is friendly, and the entertainment is...well, the entertainment may just include a dance from a sexy spirit or a ghostly game of Mahjong, so keep your eyes open and enjoy.

Having lived in Pleasanton all my life, I have been to the Gay Nineties Pizza Parlor a lot. It is one of the best pizzas in town and many people go there to eat pizza and drink beer on Friday nights. I was there on a Saturday. There were a lot of people there watching a basketball game. I was looking over at the TV by the bar and there were glasses on the bar and I thought I saw one move along the bar. I told my buddy what I saw and he just said I had drunk too much beer. I called him a (deleted) and went back to watching the game.

Our pizza came and we began eating and from the corner of my eye I saw another glass slide across the bar. I told my buddy again and this time he laughed at me, but I told him to keep his eye on the bar to see if it would happen again. It took about a half-hour, but another glass went across the bar and this time my buddy saw it too. The look on his face was funny, so I got to laugh at him. We found out when we ordered more beer and asked the girl about it that the place was haunted. I never knew this in all the times I went there before. It was cool and I hope it happens again.

~ Jason Cisneros

GAY NINETIES PIZZA COMPANY

288 Main Street
Pleasanton, CA 94566
925-846-2520
www.gayninetiespizza.com

Odd Fellows Cemetery, Pleasanton, California.

Pleasanton Pioneer Cemetery

On January 17, 1877, with only six members, Odd-Fellows Lodge #255 was organized. Within nine years, they had purchased a plot of land and the Odd-Fellows Cemetery was created. The first reported burial was a man named Peek on May 2, 1886. The plot was purchased for the price of $6.00 the next day by J. M. Peek, Esq. Although there are many tombstones with earlier dates, it is believed those may have come as relocations from other cemeteries. Looking at the markers in the cemetery and driving around the area, one will notice that many of the street names bear the same names on the gravestones, such as Ed Kinney, former mayor of Pleasanton. The markers vary in size, from the giant crypt of the Schween family, to the tiny brick-sized marker of a 64-year resident and undertaker who died in 1925.

At some point in its history, Odd-Fellows Cemetery changed its name to Pleasanton Memorial Gardens and, when the Lodge disbanded in 1999, the cemetery, now run by the Livermore Lodge, was headed for decay. Many of the interred began to be surrounded by broken and crumbling concrete, dead or dying trees and grass, roadways that were not maintained, and a sub-par irrigation system. The Livermore Lodge simply did not have the money needed for the proper upkeep of the property.

As the cemetery began to decompose, complaints from family members of those buried there began to mount; most of these complaints were directed toward the City of Pleasanton. Because of this, Livermore Lodge #219 offered to sell the

The most prominent resting places in the cemetery.

Nighttime is when the spirits come out and gather.

My roommate Caitlyn and I had been living in Pleasanton for some time and had never really noticed this small, dirt cemetery before. We had walked around during the day once we found it, but hadn't really done an actual investigation there. Our team was in town for an investigation, which was cancelled earlier that day, and we needed something to do. I suggested we check out the cemetery. We arrived about 9:30. The gates were open; apparently, they never close, so we drove up the hill and parked by the old mausoleums. Though there were six of us, we stayed together and moved toward some small tombs. We didn't know it at the time, but almost from the first we were getting EVPs on our recorders. We received direct answers to questions and a greeting from at least one spirit in response to us introducing ourselves. Unfortunately, all of this went unknown until playback. We recorded someone speaking French and an unwarranted "yes, its evil" that we still cannot understand. As exciting as all of these voices were, it pales to the knowledge that at least two of our group witnessed a full-body apparition. We were walking down the main road toward the gates when Cait stopped and asked, "Did you see that kid?" Our friend Max looked at her and said, "Good, I thought I was the only one who saw him." Both Cait and Max stated they saw a kid who seemed to be about 10 to 12 years old sitting on a gravestone along the road. As we approached, the child got up, walked across the road, and disappeared. Since none of us had ever seen a full-body spirit before, we were a bit skeptical. We had seen other shadows that evening, including what we thought was a tall man walking near the gate earlier, and figured it was just our eyes playing tricks on us. We decided to look for another possibility, but the only thing we could find was a tombstone for an 11-year-old boy named Scotty near where the child seemed to have vanished.

About a year later, Cait and I, along with another member of our group, were back up in the Bay Area for another investigation and thought it would be fun to go back to Pleasanton Cemetery. When we got there, we decided to try to find the gravesite of the young boy we had seen before, but were having trouble locating his marker. We investigated other sections of the cemetery, but wherever we went, we were on the lookout for this young man's grave. The place seemed to have a different vibe going this time – it didn't "feel" as active. We decided to look one last time for Scotty's grave and then call it a night. We went back to the main road of the cemetery. When we stopped to get our bearings, Brian said, "Hey, is that someone sitting on a headstone over there?". Cait and I turned to where he was pointing and sure enough it looked like a child sitting on a gravestone. As soon as we moved in the direction of this person, he seemed to jump down and duck behind the marker. We thought someone else might be in the cemetery and didn't want to be seen. We kept a close eye on the spot and had a good field of view; we didn't see anyone leave. After making sure no one else nearby, I glanced down at the headstone the person had hidden behind – it was Scotty's. To this day, Cait, Brian, and I believe that whom we saw was Scotty showing us again where he was buried so as to say hello and welcome back.

~ Laurel Blackwell

property to the city for $1. However, one of the concerned family members formed a not-for-profit group, incorporated as Pleasanton Pioneer Cemetery, Inc. The group estimates that the cost of upkeep for the property will be about $25,000 a year — money that is hard to come by. They were also informed by the state that there are certain obstacles to an individual taking over a cemetery, including having to retain the services of a certified cemetery operator and funding an endowment with a minimum of $100,000. While doing research, the group discovered municipalities are exempt from the same regulations and turned to the city for help. Having secured Catholic Funeral and Cemetery Services for the operations and record-keeping, on September 5, 2006, the City Council approved and a few months later changed the name to the Pleasanton Pioneer Cemetery.

Paranormal Activity

Planet Paranormal Investigations does not usually investigate cemeteries, but after seeing this beautiful, old, resting place, we decided to check it out. What we found was a place that seemed alive with the dead. We captured many EVPs and several of our group spotted the apparition of a young boy sitting on a gravestone; when approached, this boy got up, walked away, and disappeared. There also seemed to be a figure that was noticed several times walking across the roadway, but when anyone would go looking for him no one was found. Some of the EVPs captured were that of a girl saying "Hi," a girl saying "I can help you," and someone speaking French right after a group member said, "I have a tremendous urge to speak French." There were also numerous whispers caught. We consider this location to have moderately high to high paranormal activity. As I stated at the beginning, we do not usually investigate cemeteries due to the fact that we wish to be respectful of a person's final resting place — a resting place that a spirit more often than not has no connection to. If you decide to visit this or any cemetery, please remember that respect should always be given not only to the dead, but also to the families they left behind.

PLEASANTON PIONEER CEMETERY

5780 Sunol Boulevard
Pleasanton, CA 94566
925-462-2140

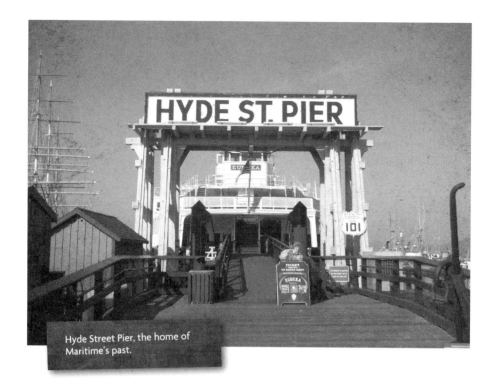

Hyde Street Pier, the home of Maritime's past.

San Francisco Maritime Museum

The San Francisco Maritime Museum is one of those places that defy explanation. In a city that embodies the ghosts of the past, this collection of ships on the Hyde Street Pier is most likely one of the most haunted places on the peninsula. At least three of these floating pieces of history are said to still house their former crew members or passengers — and these spirits seem to not be shy in letting you know they are still walking among the living, even though they themselves are not.

The square rigger *Balclutha* (once the *Star of Alaska*), the steam tug *Hercules*, and the old ferryboat *Eureka* are moored right next to each other along the pier and each had a different job and each a different story to tell. These three unique ships may have all played a part in the development of San Francisco in separate ways, but once they came together in this museum setting they each became linked to one another by way of their paranormal activity as much as by their history.

Balclutha

The *Balclutha* was built in 1886 in the city of Glasgow, Scotland. It is somewhat unclear if she was named after the town of Balclutha in New Zealand or if her name comes from *Baile Chluaidh,* which means "city on the Clyde" in Gaelic. Whichever is the case, she is a wonderful example of ship-building in the late nineteenth century.

The *Balclutha* is a 301-foot, three-masted, square-rigged windjammer that sailed on her maiden voyage in January of 1887 from Cardiff, Wales. Flying under the British flag, she was laden with 2,500 tons of coal bound for the west coast port of San Francisco. After 140 days at sea and the first rounding of what would become seventeen trips around Cape Horn in thirteen years, Captain Constable eased *Balclutha* to the wharf along the Barbary Coast district of the famous city by the bay.

With a crew of twenty-six men and eight officers, the *Balclutha* would sail to many world ports under her English banner, carrying spice and rice from Burma, wool from Australia and New Zealand, Scotch whiskey to Chile and the United States, and general heavy cargo to such far-flung Pacific ports as Hawaii and China. In 1899, the ship was transferred to Hawaiian registry and for three years carried lumber from Washington State to Australia; then, on the return trip, the *Balclutha* would load coal to be delivered to the United States. In all, the windjammer carried just over 1.5 million board feet of lumber to be used to build the cities of the lower continent. The *Balclutha* has the distinction of being the last ship to carry the flag of the Hawaiian Kingdom.

In 1901, the Congress of the United States passed an act that granted the *Balclutha* registry as an American ship. This allowed the ship to travel between U.S. ports unhindered; shortly after the act was passed, the Alaska Packers Association chartered her to carry men and supplies between San Francisco and Alaska. The *Balclutha* would continue in this capacity until, in 1904, she ran aground on Sitkin Island, near Kodiak, Alaska. The ship was deemed too damaged for repairs and was left to the sea. The Alaska Packers Association, however, saw an opportunity and purchased the *Balclutha* for a mere $500. After extensive repairs and a renaming to *Star of Alaska* (all APA ships had a *Star* prefix attached to their names), the ship was ready for a new mission.

After purchase by the Alaska Packers, the ship was upgraded to carry more than two hundred men, with additional bunks added in the "tween" deck to carry Chinese cannery workers and the poop deck extended to carry Italian and Scandinavian fishermen. After the modifications were complete, the *Star of Alaska* began sailing from San Francisco, carrying cannery workers and returning with her holds full of canned salmon. During the winter months, the ship was ported in California and would set sail as soon as the weather allowed and make as many trips as possible during the rest of the year. In September 1930, the *Star of Alaska* was finally retired.

Purchased in 1934 by Frank Kissinger and renamed once again as *Pacific Queen*, the ship became a tourist attraction by traveling up and down the West Coast in the guise of a pirate ship. She was featured in the original *Mutiny on the Bounty* film, but Kissinger allowed the ship to slowly deteriorate over time and was finally forced to berth her as unsafe.

In 1954, the *Pacific Queen* was acquired by the San Francisco Maritime Museum and the long process of restoring the ship to her former glory began. Shipwrights studied original plans, docents solicited funds and material, and slowly the ship was brought back to life. Once complete, she was rechristened the *Balclutha* and began her long and still-continuing career as a museum gem. Formally given over to the National Park Service in 1978 and designated a National Historic Landmark in 1985, the *Balclutha* today sits at the end of the Hyde Street Pier and harkens back to the days of sailing the open seas and the romance of a past long gone. However, even though the past may be gone, some of those who sailed her more than a hundred years ago may still remain.

Steam Tug Hercules

The *Hercules* was built in 1907 in New Jersey for the Shipowners and Merchants Tugboat Company of San Francisco. From the moment she left the docks in Camden, this oil-fired steam tug began setting maritime records that still stand today. Reaching the west coast of the United States from the east in 1907 meant transiting the Straits of Magellan. The *Hercules* made the trip while towing her sister ship, the *Goliah,* which held extra fuel, water, and supplies for the long voyage. Once she reached San Francisco, the two tugs joined the "Red Stack Fleet" of the company and the *Hercules* began her long career traveling up and down the west coast and Hawaii.

The tug's first job was as an oceangoing tug assisting sailing ships heading north. The prevailing winds would often hinder the masted ships from making headway and the tugs were needed to tow the sailing ships to ports as far away as Washington State. On the return trips, the *Hercules* would pick up barges laden with millions of board feet of lumber headed for ports south as far as San Diego and even across the open ocean to Hawaiian ports. On these long overseas voyages, the deck was often awash and because of her deep narrow hull she rode low in the water and life was uncomfortable at best and deadly at worst. The *Hercules* was also instrumental in the construction of the Panama Canal by towing a giant steel structure used for closing the canal entrance and by making numerous trips transporting equipment and lumber needed for completion of the massive project.

In 1924, the *Hercules* was bought by Western Pacific Railroad and with this purchase her open ocean days were at an end. The railroad used the ship as a railcar ferry transiting the bay between San Francisco, Oakland, and Alameda. The ship would continue in this capacity until 1957 when the diesel-powered train ferry *Las Palmas* replaced her. The *Hercules* was kept in port as a backup until 1961 when she was retired. The great tug would languish, tied up at the wharf rusting, until it was decided to sell her for scrap.

The thought of this great ship being destroyed was too much for some and in 1975 the San Francisco Maritime State Historic Park stepped in and saved the tug from the cutter's torch. Funds being tight, restoration was slow until, in 1977, the National Parks Service took over and completed the work. In 1986, the *Hercules* was designated a National Historic Landmark and is part of the Historic American Engineering Record's Maritime Project. Today, the *Hercules* is completely restored and operational. She regularly steams around San Francisco Bay with a volunteer crew as a prime example of strong American work ethics and quality construction of a time long ago. Although her crew seems to be all volunteer, it would seem that there are still some of the *Hercules'* original seamen that are still aboard making sure she is being treated well and with the respect she deserves.

The mighty *Hercules* steam tug ready for a job.

I have lived in San Francisco my entire life and simply love the Fishermen's Wharf area of the city. My boyfriend Stanley and I went there on a Saturday morning to spend the day just wandering around and enjoying the atmosphere, watching the funny things tourists do, and to just be together. After having lunch at Loris Diner in Ghirardelli Square, we decided to head down to Hyde Street Pier.

Hyde Street Pier is also called the Maritime Museum because there are four or five ships docked along the wharf. I have been on board these ships many times, but have never had any kind of paranormal activity happen, even though I was aware of the stories regarding a couple of the ships. These stories hadn't even crossed my mind when we boarded the old Tugboat.

We were walking around the old tug and had started up on the bridge deck, then made our way down to the main deck of the ship. My boyfriend said that even though we had just eaten, the smell coming from the kitchen was so good that it was making him hungry again. We couldn't tell what it was that we were smelling, but I agreed that it did smell delicious and wondered if the cook might be able to give me a recipe. As we headed for the kitchen, we started hearing the sound of men laughing and having a good time and figured that they were who the meal must have been planned for. The noise got louder as we neared, but when we turned and looked in where the sound was coming from all the noise stopped; we looked, but there was no one in the room and the smell of the great cooking stopped as well. Both of us just looked into the room for a minute, then at each other. When our eyes met, Stanley and I got silly grins on our faces and hugged each other — we both realized that we had just heard and smelled ghosts.

~ Brenda Childress

The *Balclutha* in all her glory.

The stately *Eureka* still recalls the time when ships were the transports of the new motorcars that wanted to cross the bay.

The *Balclutha*'s passengers always sailed in luxury, if not comfort.

Paddle Wheel Steamboat Eureka (Ukiah)

Built in 1890 in Tiburon, California, the side-wheel paddle steamer *Ukiah* is today the only wooden hull, walking-beam engine ferry in the United States that is still preserved in floating condition. She was built for the North Pacific Railroad Company to carry commuters and railcars between Tiburon and San Francisco. The commuters were carried during the day, while the railcars were transported by night, but with the advent of the automobile and its growing popularity, by 1907 the company decided to move the *Ukiah* to the Sausalito-San Francisco route, which left from the new ferry building along the Embarcadero.

The *Ukiah* continued transporting autos and their passengers until the United States entered WWI, at which time she was pressed into service carrying railroad cars that were loaded with munitions and supplies for the war effort. She worked this duty for three years and because of the need for more and more war supplies the railcars were often overloaded, which put a huge strain on the ship's machinery and hull. Because of this, when the war was over, the United States government was obligated to completely rehab the ship. The damage was so severe that everything above the water line needed to be replaced, which took two years to complete. Because of the extent of the repairs, it was decided that the ferry would be given a new name along with her new superstructure and hull and she was re-christened the *Eureka*.

During reconstruction, the size of the *Eureka* grew to accommodate 2,300 passengers and 120 automobiles, and in 1923, she continued her Sausalito-San Francisco commuter runs. Her primary role was to transport passengers, with few cars making the transit; nevertheless, because she was the largest ferry in the fleet, she was scheduled for the busiest runs of the day and often made extra trips on Sundays to carry the many travelers heading across the bay for drives up the coast. Because of the large commuter population, it was decided to upgrade the ferry with numerous amenities to make travel across the bay more comfortable. Now included in the upper deck seating area were a magazine stand and a full-service restaurant. The *Eureka* was the finest ship of her type afloat and first-class all the way. The completion of the Golden Gate Bridge, however, spelled doom for ferry service in the bay, with many routes being cut and others greatly reduced. By 1941, Northwestern Pacific abandoned ferry service altogether.

Over the intervening years, the *Eureka* performed odd jobs. During WWII, she transported troops from camp to debarkation stations throughout the bay, moved railcars from various locations, and even hauled cargo from different docks. In 1957, she snapped a crank pin within her engine, was towed to port, and retired from service. There was never a doubt about what her next job would be; in the following year, 1958, the *Eureka* proudly joined the fleet at the National Maritime Museum and today is still afloat at the spot where she picked up so many passengers and cars at the Hyde Street Pier. It is fitting perhaps that she resides at one of her main ports of debarkation, because at least one of her past passengers still seems to enjoy her grace and beauty, even though he has long ago passed from this earthly realm.

Paranormal Activity

Although the steamboat *Eureka* is the most famous boat at the museum, it is also the least active of the three haunted ships. Over the years, many visitors have seen an old man on the passenger deck sitting in the pews closest to the bay. This man is wearing what appears to be an old style overcoat and breasted suit out of a "Roaring Twenties" movie, right down to his driving cap. This gentleman is often preceded by the slight scent of cologne and smoke. No one knows exactly who this person is, as there are no reports of anyone passing on the ship, but what is known is that when approached he will glance up, give an impish smile, and disappear.

The *Hercules,* by contrast to the ferryboat, has any number of reported ghost sightings. The type of work that the tug performed in its lifetime was arduous, as well as dangerous. Men were often washed overboard during storms and injured or killed going about their duties. Because of this, it should be no surprise that the *Hercules* would be haunted.

Tourists have reported strange cold spots suddenly manifesting in various places all over the old tug. One couple from Germany was up in the bridge area and was impressed by the re-enactor who was portraying the captain of the vessel. When they mentioned the wonderful job that the man did to one of the Rangers on duty and found out that the museum had never employed anyone for that job, they were as perplexed as the employee as to whom it could have been. Going back to the tug, they could find no one matching the description of the man they had met and no other visitor could recall having seen the man.

One of the perks of life on an oceangoing tug was the food. No expense was spared to give the crew delicious meals while onboard and as such the galley was a gathering place for the officers and crew while not on duty. Reports have been coming in for years of people smelling the aroma of bread and other delicacies coming from the kitchen, as well as the sound of men enjoying themselves in the common area. All sounds and smells cease when the areas are approached.

Of all the boats, the tall ship *Balclutha* is, by far, considered to be the most haunted. Many stories have emerged about spectral crewmen seeming to appear out of nowhere, some gesturing at visitors, others just staring and then slowly fading into nothingness. As with her sister ship, the *Star of India* in San Diego, the *Balclutha* has had reports of tourists being touched, pushed, tugged, and having their hair pulled. There are no firm conclusions of who may be responsible for these manifestations or why, but it is assumed that a younger crewman, perhaps a cabin boy or crew steward, may have passed sometime during the schooner's long career and, as children often do, is playing in a bid for attention.

Another area where much activity has been reported is the officers' billets. In the surgeon's room, visitors have heard moans as if someone is sick or in pain, and in the Captain's quarters guests have reported seeing what appears to be a man in uniform around a map, as if plotting a course. When approached, the specter vanishes without a trace. Cold spots, areas around the ship where the hairs on a person's arm will suddenly rise up, and orbs being photographed with regularity are all common occurrences aboard the ship as well.

Planet Paranormal was able to investigate these three ships on two different occasions. We didn't catch any evidence on either, but we did have one personal experience aboard the *Balclutha*. While on the middle deck, one of our members began to feel apprehensive and had the feeling of being watched. This happened for only the briefest of moments and then simply went away. It is for this reason alone that we give a rating of mild haunting activity.

Life at sea, no matter what type of vessel or what era you sailed, was never easy. The ocean is a hard taskmaster and a person could find himself or herself at peril in an instant. Because of this, those who went to sea learned to live life to the fullest and with a gusto that land lubbers may never understand. Keeping this in mind, is it any wonder that the crew of these ships may be unable or unwilling to understand that they are no longer part of the living? These three wonderful ships are a link to our history and who we are as a nation and those that remain aboard are surely part of that storied past, so if you find yourself in San Francisco, visit the Maritime Museum and learn about the Golden Age of California sea life from one of the knowledgeable docents...or maybe you will be lucky enough to learn from the actual crew who still remain on look out.

SAN FRANCISCO MARITIME MUSEUM

499 Jefferson Street
San Francisco, CA 94109
(On the Hyde Street Pier)

The *USS Hornet* still on duty.

USS Hornet Museum

The keel for the *USS Hornet* was originally laid down as the *USS Kearsarge* on August 3, 1942. However, because the seventh *Hornet* (CV-8) was sunk at the Battle of Santa Cruz on October 26, 1942, the hull of CV-12 was renamed *Hornet* in honor of the ship that launched the Doolittle raid against Tokyo. The name *Kearsarge* is still stamped onto her keel plate, thus she became the eighth ship to bear the name *Hornet*. Built at Newport News shipyards in Virginia, the *Hornet* was one of the twenty-four famed *Essex* class aircraft carriers built during the war. The *Hornet* was also one of the most decorated ships in the U.S. Navy. Able to carry up to one hundred aircraft, she bristled with anti-aircraft and anti-ship guns ranging in size from 20mm up to 5" cannons; 121 guns ringed her decks in all. She was launched on August 30, 1943, and commissioned November 29th of that same year. With a full complement of men and machines, she displaced 36,380 tons and had a range of 20,000 nautical miles in her WWII configuration. She had eight boilers powering four Westinghouse-geared steam turbines, which turned four shaft propellers that gave the ship a 33-knot speed.

The *Hornet* departed Pearl Harbor on March 15, 1944, and headed for the forward area combat zone, and for the next eighteen months would not again tie up to a pier. At one point, she was only forty nautical miles from mainland Japan. She came under air attack fifty-nine times, but was never hit by the bombs of the Japanese. While the Japanese were trying to sink the *Hornet*, her aircraft was destroying 1,410 of the enemy's planes. Only the *Essex* herself would exceed this record. Ten pilots of the *Hornet* would achieve ace-in-a-day status and her Hellcats would also hold the record of knocking down seventy-two enemy planes in one day and 255 in that same month. The *Hornet* pilots were also responsible for sinking or heavily damaging 1,269,710 tons of shipping and had a critical role in the destruction of the Japanese super battleship *Yamato*.

After eighteen months of dueling it out with the Imperial Japanese Navy's ships and aircraft, it was the sea herself that caused the great ship *Hornet* to finally return to port. On June 5, 1945, a typhoon hit the Pacific Ocean and the *Hornet* and her crew were subjected to 120-mph winds and sixty-foot high waves that washed over her decks. This was the second such storm that the *Hornet* had sailed through that year and caused twenty-four feet of the ship's bow to buckle and collapse. The next day, the *Hornet* launched her planes off the stern of the ship to be sent to other carriers and then proceeded to the west coast of the United States. She arrived at the docks of Alameda Naval Base on July 8th.

The war would be over by the time the *Hornet* was repaired, but her mission would not be. Following her stay at Alameda, the ship took part in the so-called "magic carpet" cruises that returned troops home from the Pacific war. She made trips from both the Marianas and Hawaii — five in all — in what was, as the crew recalls, "The best missions of the war." She returned from the Pacific once again to San Francisco in February 1946 and was subsequently decommissioned on January 15, 1947, becoming a member of the reserve fleet.

The *Hornet* would not remain in mothballs for long and was recommissioned just long enough to sail to New York to undergo conversion to an attack carrier. Re-commissioned CVA-12 on September 11, 1953, she spent time training in the Caribbean Sea and then set sail on an around-the-world cruise as a show of American naval power. The *Hornet* was on station after China shot down a British passenger aircraft and helped search for survivors, and her planes would shoot down two attacking communist fighters threatening the operation. In January 1956, the *Hornet* entered the Puget Sound Naval Shipyard to undergo her final modernization, which included the angled flight deck that you see today. Again, she was given a new designation, that of CVS-12.

After a stint in the waters off Vietnam, the *Hornet* spent time training and again went worldwide to protect American interests. In 1969, she sailed from Hawaii for one of the most historic missions of her career. On July 24, 1969, with President Nixon on board, the *Hornet* recovered Neil Armstrong, Michael Collins, and Edwin "Buzz" Aldrin after returning from the first mission to land on the surface of the moon. The place where these pioneers walked is marked even today on her hangar deck next to the quarantine station where the President greeted them. The *Hornet*

What's left of an F4 on the hangar deck.

The *Apollo 11* was recovered on the flight deck of the *USS Hornet*.

The medical ward is one of the most haunted places on the *Hornet*.

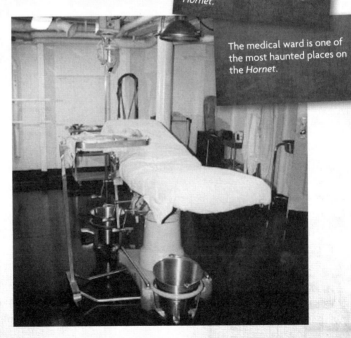

was also on hand to recover the men of *Apollo 12* after their splashdown from the moon. She then sailed to Puget Sound Navel shipyard, where, on June 26, 1970, the *Hornet* was decommissioned for the last time and was once again mothballed. On July 25, 1989, the *Hornet* was stricken from the Naval Vessel Registry. In 1991, she was given the designation as being a National Historic Landmark and the long process of turning her into a living museum began.

After years of loving care and devotion by a group of volunteers, the *Hornet* again started a new mission — as the *USS Hornet* Museum on October 17, 1998 — and received California Historic Landmark designation the following year. Her record is one of the most distinguished in the Navy. She was one of only nine carriers to be awarded the Presidential unit citation, one of only five to receive the Navy unit commendation award, and the only ship to have an official presidential seal. Today, the Navy's F/A-18 strike fighter carries on the name and tradition of the great ships that once bore the name "Hornet."

Paranormal Activity

In her twenty-seven years of active duty, three hundred people lost their lives aboard ship. An aircraft carrier is one of the most dangerous places to work. Crewmen have fallen overboard, been chewed up by spinning propellers, sucked into jet engines, and ripped apart by snapped arresting wires. Bombs and other high explosives going off on deck and fire have killed many men. With all the drama and tragedy associated with a carrier at war, is it any wonder this great ship should be haunted?

Reports of paranormal activity started almost immediately after the restoration of the *Hornet* began. Workers would tell of hearing hatchway doors slamming shut in areas where no one was working, tools disappearing for long stretches of time, only to reappear where they had been left, items falling off shelves or desks for no apparent reason, and objects scooting across the floor as if being pushed by unseen hands. There were even reports of transparent sailors being spotted going about their work as if the ship were still at sea. While walking through the hangar deck, one volunteer remembers hearing what sounded like work being done on an aircraft and could hear the mechanics talking about the work they were doing, what parts they would need, how long it would take to get the plane back in the air, and even talking about what they were going to do once they got back home.

During group sleep-overs, people have seen shadows passing by the bunks and have heard whispered conversations. There is a bunk area where people's shoes would disappear or be moved when they wake up; this area is close to the surgical/ hospital ward and people have heard the sounds of medical staff going about the work of healing the sick or injured. Some areas have been closed to the overnight program due to activity, especially the bunks near the fo'c'sel (forward).

Planet Paranormal had the opportunity to spend the night on this great ship during an event with Todd Sheets's Nightwatch group. We did not record any evidence or have any personal experiences, but this may have been a result of some confusion with the ship's personnel about our role of investigating the ship. It is for that reason alone that we give the *Hornet* a rating of mild paranormal activity.

The *Hornet* is a reminder that the cost of freedom is vigilance and the will to act when diplomacy fails. It is a monument to the bravery and dedication of the men and women of our Armed Services and of the sacrifices they have made on our behalf. A trip to this ship is a way to pay respect to these heroes and to learn a small part of this nation's history. While there, if you happen to catch sight of one of these true Americans, don't be scared and don't run away. Look them in the eye and say with conviction, "Thank you and God bless you." Let them know that they are remembered and maybe they will continue to watch over the great ship with the same dedication they showed in life, but then, they are already letting us know that they are still serving our nation and us and watching over this magnificent ship.

The *USS Hornet* is a piece of my family's history, as my grandfather was aboard during WW2. He was a gunner's mate and from what I heard he was under fire many times especially during the Okinawa invasion. I was delighted to hear that the ship was a museum attraction open to the public and as we were going to San Francisco for vacation, I planned on taking my family to see the ship that "grandpa" fought the war on.

We were staying by the piers in San Francisco and the *Bart* was nearby, so we headed out on a train and then a cab and got to the pier where the ship was docked, but were a bit under-whelmed by what we saw. The place looked as if it was a deserted storage site for unwanted scrap metal, but we were still excited to go on the ship, as it was a piece of naval history. Once on board, we were glad we had come. The *Apollo 11* exhibit was something we had not expected and never knew about and we were simply amazed that a WW2 [ship] would have an escalator on board.

We went below deck and looked at the wardroom, medical center, the forward chain hold area, and then up on deck and to the bridge. The kids were having a great time, pretending to be "army men," and playing as if they were the captains on the boat. My husband and I were examining the old charts they had on display in the chart room when I heard the boys in the next room talking to someone. I looked back and noticed a man in a navy uniform seemed to be explaining some of the equipment to our sons. He looked at me and smiled as if to say, "It's OK, I got them." I smiled back and went back to my husband. I figured it was a docent and that he was just keeping the boys busy while at the sametime making sure they weren't getting into any trouble.

My husband and I wandered around on the small bridge for a bit, gratified that the docent was entertaining the kids and we had a bit of free time to ourselves, although we were beginning to feel a little guilty. We took a few more minutes, then went back to collect our children from the poor man who had been watching them for the last half-hour or so. We thanked the man who just nodded and smiled, tipped his hat, and walked away. I watched him enter another room, but before he went any farther he turned, smiled again, and then just simply vanished. I stood there for a second with my mouth hitting the floor and then rushed into the room the man had vanished from. The room had no other door; there was no way for the man to have disappeared from the room, but that's exactly what had happened. He was not in the room when I looked.

I went back and told my husband what had happened and of course he did not believe me. I then asked the children if they had any problems with the gentleman who had spent so much time with them and they just told me that he was a nice old guy that told them a lot of cool stories about the ship. I was and am to this day scared about what could have happened to my boys if this man had indeed been a ghost. My husband keeps telling me that I must have taken my eyes off of the guy long enough for him to have gone down a different hallway, but even if it had been the ghost of a sailor...then he had just been looking out for his ship and crewmates while also making sure their legacy and history lived on by teaching our kids. Small comfort to this mother, but I see my husband's point.

~ Shirley Summers

USS HORNET MUSEUM

Pier 3 Alameda Point
Alameda, CA 94501
510-521-8448
www.uss-hornet.org

Wolfe Manor is not only haunted, but even looks the part.

Wolfe Manor

Some time in the early 1900s, two men, Tony Andriotti and his brother-in-law, Gust Spiropulos, had a race to see who could build the largest, most elaborate and luxurious house possible. The two men started the competition next door to each other, with Tony building on what was most likely his stepfather, Frank Fierro's, property, although he presumably did not assume possession until sometime after 1920. Tony seems to have won this race, as the house that now sits on Clovis Avenue can attest.

After Tony's death sometime around 1930, his wife, Della, may have lost the property due to financial pressure and the advent of the Great Depression; however, the details are sketchy. It is believed that Della sold the property to one Jens Hansen, who, at one time, was listed as living next door to Gust and Rosie (Andriotti) Spiropulos. Mr. Hansen held onto the house until 1942, when he sold it to Mr. Lee Brashears and his wife, who converted the house into the Clovis Avenue Sanitarium. A hospital wing was added onto the back of the house and a three-bedroom home and three-car garage were built on the property to the south for the owners. This garage was later converted into a laundry room. The property seems to have remained so until sometime in the early 1970s, when it was converted into the now infamous Clovis Convalescent Hospital. I say "infamous" because while operating as a

"Mary's" room is arguably the most haunted room at Wolfe Manor.

Planet Paranormal ready for action!

retirement facility, the place became a cramped, overcrowded place devoted more to money than care for the elderly. This manifested in that so many people were crammed into the rooms of the main house that one would have to walk over the bodies of the dead to reach the live patients. Neighbors reported screams and moans coming from the hospital at all hours of the day and night and ambulance drivers tell of not being able to get their gurneys into the rooms to remove the bodies. The basement was set up as a temporary morgue due to its low temperatures, but even so, the deceased could remain there for days or even weeks on end. Due to this deplorable behavior, the county closed the facility down in the late 1980s. Records show that after 1986 the property was owned by an O. Garcia. What his plans for the hospital may have been is not known, but in 1992 the property was again sold, this time to the present owner, Todd Wolfe.

Mr. Wolfe bought the place to turn it into a "haunted house" attraction in 1996 and successfully ran it as such for years. He renamed the house the Andleberry Estate (a fictional name) and recruited students from Clovis East High School's drama department to work in the house. Mr. Wolfe's generosity in donating funds allowed the school to produce many shows and the time spent working at the "Estate" gave the students valuable experience in work and drama.

The Andleberry was voted the #1 haunted attraction in California for a number of years; however, in 2004 the city of Clovis gave in to neighbors' demands and closed the haunted house for good. Todd Wolfe would not be easily put off and opened the manor for private ghost tours while planning a renovation for a haunted luxury hotel. This would involve tearing down the existing hospital wing and moving the residence house and garage to a new location while leaving the original mansion where it sits. After moving the buildings and drawing up the plans, Mr. Wolfe has found that the wheels of bureaucracy, with their red tape and personal bias, can grind slowly. To help make ends meet at the manor, Mr. Wolfe kept up the tours and created Wolfe Manor live podcast and began using the house to help train the local police and fire departments in urban rescue. As of this writing, it is believed that the go-ahead for the hotel has been granted and construction should begin soon.

It was only three days since my mother had passed and being a tour guide at Wolfe Manor I wasn't a stranger to the weird goings on there, nor was I a stranger to the theory that if one is sick or feeling down that you can be vulnerable to the possibility of spirit attachment. So, after another long day of tours I was exhausted. After making my final rounds through the house looking for any guests that may have been left inside or who were hiding looking to be alone in the house, I went outside to have a smoke. The thought of my mother's passing was weighing heavy on me on as I tried to relax on the porch. My mother was a paranormal investigator herself and I guess you could say I inherited that passion from her side of the family. A close friend,

Jen, came out on the porch and told me to go home; she said that I should be with my family and explained that my loss might open a doorway to the spirit world that could allow an attachment from the other side.

The following day, the tours started up and as usual we were quite busy throughout the day. We were all pretty excited because right after the tours ended we would be shooting one of our web shows. At this time [2006], paranormal webcasts were pretty rare and we knew we had a lot of work to get the Manor ready. After the last tour, Terry, Todd, Jen, and myself, along with our producer, Brandon, worked to prepare the house and we all had the feeling that the Manor and her spirits were not happy about what we were planning on doing.

An hour into the show, I thought it would be funny to crawl up into a crawlspace in the basement so Brandon could set Terry up for a scare. The plan was to get Terry near the crawlspace and then when I heard the code word, "rose," I would reach out and grab him. I could hear Terry coming and then Brandon say, "Hello Rose, are you here?" so I reached out to grab him and something grabbed my ankles and pulled me back before I could grab Terry. I had heard of spirits touching and pushing, but never a yank like I felt here. I came out of the crawlspace gasping and scared; well, terrified is a better word. I fell to the floor and almost cracked my head on the concrete floor. To make matters worse, I had lost one of my shoes and my pants had somehow been pulled down to my ankles.

As I lay in the hospital, I tried to think of a logical explanation for what had happened. Was there another person in there? A cat, or did I just get caught on something in the small space? I have watched the footage many times and still can't explain what grabbed me that day. MOM?

I returned weeks later to that spot, alone at midnight with a flashlight in hand, and crawled back to the spot I had occupied that night. Laying there on the cool dirt, I stared up at the old sub-floor and all I can do is talk to my mom. Weird? Yeah, I guess, but I did get some kind of closure. As I climbed safely out, I noticed something shiny in the dirt; it was my mom's rosary, which I had lost years before she passed. She had given it to me to protect me from whatever it was she thought lived in the basement of the haunted Wolfe Manor.

~ Scott Greunwald

Paranormal Activity

Planet Paranormal was privileged enough to be able to investigate this wonderfully haunted house with its courteous and fun-loving staff, and we were amazed at the level of activity. While there, we caught the sound of gurneys moving down the hallways, phantom footsteps following us up the staircase, lights shining in rooms with no electricity, whistling in response to others' whistles or singing, and the sighting of an apparition (only from the waist down). One of our investigators even had a spectral "hello" spoken into their ear. Other reports from neighbors and guests at the house include disembodied voices, the sound of children playing, a woman screaming and pleading "get me out of here," and even full-body apparitions.

We consider this location to be moderately high to high in paranormal activity, so if you ever find yourself in the town of Clovis, California, we highly recommend you stop in at Wolfe Manor or, once the hotel is finished, rent a room and have a frightfully good night.

WOLFE MANOR

2604 Clovis Avenue
Clovis, CA 93611

TOOLS OF THE TRADE

For those of you that are new to the field of paranormal investigation, I thought I would include a list of the most common "ghost hunting" tools so that if you decide to go to these locations and want to take some equipment, you would have an idea of what you might need and a rough idea of what it might cost you. I have omitted most specialized tools of the trade as they are quite costly and need a degree of commitment if purchasing.

Camera: Any camera will work to take pictures of ghostly occurrences. However, if you are using film, make sure that it has an ISO rating to be able to handle the dark corners of the site. Digital is more convenient and less expensive in the long run due to not having to pay for development of your pictures. Check all of your photos carefully and try not to imagine a spirit in the picture if one is not there. Matrixing is a common mistake of novices. Most groups are more than happy to look at your photos and can give you an expert opinion as to whether you actually caught a spirit on film. The cost of cameras vary widely, but I am sure that most of you have one that will work just fine.

Voice Recorder: Voice recorders are used to capture EVP and other audio. There are many ideas on what quality a recorder should be; however, I have found that a digital recorder in the $30 to $70 price range seems to work just fine. Many new MP3 players also have voice-recording capability and that is also fine. Tape recorders and mini recorders will work, but having to carry extra tapes and the cost of said tapes should be considered.

EMF Meter: Used to detect fluctuations in the electromagnetic field of an area, these can range in price from a basic LED bar readout model costing $20 to one with all the bells and whistles that can exceed $250. If you plan on just being an occasional ghost hunter, I would recommend not using one. If, on the other hand, you feel you might get hooked on hunting, start with a basic digital readout model. These start at about $70 and are more than adequate. A KII meter is also a good choice (simple light bar readout) and can be purchased for about $50.

Thermometer: Used to detect changing temperatures in a room or on an object, these can range from simple mercury (not recommended) to a dual temperature recordable model that can run $200. Many people use a laser thermometer thinking that they are sampling the room temperature, but are actually recording only what the laser is hitting. It is much more effective to use an ambient air thermometer as this samples the actual air in the room. They also make dual temperature units, but, as I mentioned above, these can be much more expensive.

Camcorder/miniDV: Used to catch anomalies or spirits, miniDVs are probably the preferred medium for movie cameras among ghost hunters. The reasons for this are the fact that the tapes are small, record in digital quality, and, if using a Sony, most come equipped with a built-in night vision option. The cameras are small and light and easy to use in confined areas, stairs, and ladders. The cameras are pricey, though; they can run anywhere from $175 up to a couple thousand. An older camcorder will work, but remember, they can wear you down with the sheer weight of the camera and tapes.

Compass: This can be used as a makeshift EMF detector. When a spirit is in the area, the needle on the compass will spin. This is not a sure thing, but can be used in a pinch; and the best thing about it is that they are inexpensive.

Pendulum: These are used to detect and communicate with the spirit world. When an entity is in the area of the pendulum, it will spin. There is some speculation that the direction it spins will tell you if it is an evil or benign spirit. We do not subscribe to that theory; therefore, we will leave it to you to explore. The pendulum may also be used to help communicate with an entity by asking it to spin the device clockwise for yes and counter-clockwise for no. Ask a spirit to spin the pendulum and then to stop it to prove that it is present. The cost for a pendulum can run from $5 to $75 depending on where you buy them and what the stone or crystal is made from.

Divining Rods: These metal rods are used to detect the presence of a spirit. When an entity is present, the rods will cross in front of the person holding them. You can also use them to have yes or no questions answered by having the spirit cross or uncross the rods. The cost for these rods can range from $10 to $50.

Flashlight: The use for these should need no explanation. I would say that a good flashlight should be purchased, (you don't want it to break at the wrong time). A Mini Mag is a good choice and can be purchased for around $15. If you want to preserve your night vision, then a red lens can replace the clear lens it comes with.

Batteries: You should have extra batteries for all of your equipment. Ghosts have been known to drain any electrical device in the area as a way to manifest themselves or let you know that it is present. Make sure before you arrive at your hunt that you have all the different types (A, AA, D, etc.) that your devices require and that your spare rechargeable have a full charge. It can be very frustrating to have an encounter and have no way to record it.

For those of you who just have to know what I meant by "specialized," here is a brief list:

DVR: $3,000   **Franks Box:** $500
Motion sensors: $50 and up...Each!   **Night vision digital still:** $200 and up
Infrared scope: $5,000 and up   **IR illuminators:** $100 and up

That is just a brief list of other equipment one can use to hunt. As you can see, it can get quite costly. If you decide to give ghost-hunting a go, just beware: It can be very addicting and soon you may find yourself working those extra hours in order to buy more equipment and to pay for that trip to go in search of the unknown.

HAPPY HUNTING!

Glossary of Terms

Anomaly: Any unexplained event or occurrence. An EVP is an example of a sound anomaly.

Anomalous Experience: An occurrence that cannot be explained by scientific terms.

Apparition: Considered by some to be the "Holy Grail" of paranormal evidence, this is an anomaly that appears to be that of a human in misty or transparent form. Sometimes hard to see with the naked eye, they can be made out on film or video. They can appear as a whole or partial entity with body parts missing. On even more rare occasions, apparitions have been indistinguishable from live people...there one second, gone the next.

Audible: Any sound or voice that can be heard with the human ear.

AVP: Audible Voice Phenomena is when most people present can hear a spirit audibly. Bob Davis of Planet Paranormal first coined this term.

Channeling: The ability of a medium to allow a spirit to communicate through them.

Clairaudience: The ability to hear things outside the normal range of human hearing; the ability to hear spirits.

Clairsentience: The ability to smell or feel things outside the normal range for humans; the ability to smell or feel paranormal scents and/or emotion.

Clairvoyance: The ability to see objects or events outside the normal range of humans; acute insight or perceptiveness.

Cold Spots: These are areas in a location that are markedly colder than the rest of the room. These can be stationary or may move about, may appear suddenly and vanish just as quickly. Objects are subject to this phenomena as well as the surrounding air. It is believed that spirits will use the energy in the air to manifest or to move items; this drain of the surrounding energy causes the temperatures to drop.

Ectoplasm: A substance believed to be a manifestation of spirit matter that can take the form of a white swirling mist and may be accompanied by unusual odors and on rare occasions by sounds.

EMF: An Electro Magnetic Field is the field produced by man-made and natural electricity, also known as Gauss. High EMF is known to cause feelings of unease and paranoia and can make someone feel things and hear anomalous sounds. High EMF can be associated with spirits who may be trying to manifest.

Entity: A being such as an animal or person, spirit, demon, or any other preternatural form.

EVP: The recording of a sound or voice that is not audible to the human ear. During an investigation, it is standard to hold an EVP session. Questions are asked while recording devices are active and then later the investigator will review the recording to see if any answers were recorded that were not discernible during the session itself. One technique is to ask several questions and then play back the audio while still in the location to see if any answers were given. This simulates a sort of conversation with the alleged entity. This is rare, but possible. (*1)

Fortean Phenomenon: Term used for any strange, unexplained phenomenon involving the paranormal, cryptozoological, or meteorologic. Named after American researcher and writer Charles Fort.

Ghost: This is the term used to describe any number of manifestations. People tend to lump all sorts of spirits into this category. A ghost is actually the spirit of a dead human being; a person who may not know they have passed, who is looking for something, or who is trying to get help. They usually appear as their former selves, but have also been known to change their appearance. They are not evil, but retain the personality they had while alive. Nice, mean...any and all manner of human traits. Remember that they are people and treat them as such.

Haunting: The manifestation of a spirit or spirits that remain in one place and make themselves known by the manipulation of objects or disembodied sounds or voices. Some people believe that only a place can be haunted; however, there have been cases where an entity has followed people to other locations. There have also been cases of a ghost manifesting itself in more than one location.

Hot Spot: An area of frequent paranormal activity.

IVP: Indirect Voice Phenomenon. When an entity uses the voice of a living person, the voice will usually sound slightly different and seem to be coming from thin air.

Luminous Phenomenon: Strange lights or glows, usually around objects or people.

Matrixing (pareidolia): The phenomenon of seeing a false image such as a face or glowing eyes when there is nothing to see. (*2)

OBE: Out of Body Experience.

Orb: A ball of light that usually only appears on a picture or video and seems to move around with a conscious effort. Can on occasion be seen with the naked eye. (*3)

Paranormal: That which is outside the normal range of explanation.

Parapsychology: Science that specializes in the study of psychic and paranormal phenomenon. (*4)

Phasmophobia: The fear of ghosts.

Poltergeist: A German word meaning "noisy ghost." A spirit that causes disorder and disruption, causes things to move erratically, causes loud noises, especially at night, and on occasion can cause harm to those in the area by causing objects to fly around and strike with force. (*5)

PSP: Paranormal Sound Phenomena. This is a term coined to encompass all unexplained sounds. Because the sound of a knock or tap or other such noise does not fall into the category of a "voice," we thought a more general term was in order. First coined by Guy Jackson, but advanced by Planet Paranormal as a more rounded term for all sound phenomena.

Shadow Person: An entity that looks to be in the shape of a human being, but appears in the form of a shadow. Black or gray in appearance, they have no discernible features, move very quickly, and can appear and disappear in the blink of an eye.

Spirit Photography: A ghost or entity caught on film or video. (Also see Matrixing)

Thought Form: A spirit or entity created by the power of human thought. (*6)

Vortex: A door or portal that allows entities to travel from our reality to theirs.

1: EVPs are classified as class A, class B, and class C. The most common EVPs are those rated C. The reason for this is that they are usually of such poor quality that one can hear anything they want to hear. PLPI tends to toss these, as they will NEVER be classified as evidence. Class B are better in that words, although distorted, can mostly be understood with some enhancements and cleanup from a good audio program. Class A EVPs are clear, and usually need very little cleanup to be understood.

2: Matrixing is a form of illusion caused by the human brain. If you sit in a dark room long enough and your eyes have nothing to focus on, your brain can create an image out of the little light that is present. This image can take the form of what you are thinking of at that time or one of your deepest fears. It is not real, but illusion formed by the brain.

Many people want to see a face or spirit in a mirror or photograph so badly that their mind will pick out random patterns or flaws in the photo or glass or video and form it into that which the observer wishes to see. Again, not real but illusion.

Audio Matrixing is when random noise is heard live or recorded and listened to long enough that the brain strives to make sense of what it is hearing and will start to form voice patterns that the listener can make out. Again, illusion.

So you need to be careful not to fall into this trap when you are reviewing potential evidence because if you do, then all the rest of your evidence, authentic or not, will be suspect and not taken seriously.

3: Orbs are commonly believed to be the manifestation of spirits or ghosts. It is the theory of many that these spirits use the energy around them to create the orb as a way of letting us know they are here. This is a theory that PLPI does not necessarily subscribe to. This is typically a case of either Matrixing or just plain wishful thinking. PLPI takes MANY orb pictures and can 99.9% of the time find a logical explanation for the orb. The most common are an insect or a dust particle reflecting the flash of the camera. No flash while using IR? Then what you are seeing may be IR reflection. This is not to say that the small .10 % cannot be a spirit just that we have not found any proof to suggest that it is. Too many people and groups are now saying that every photo with an orb is paranormal and this makes all the rest of their evidence suspect. Please do not fall into this trap; look carefully and be objective when analyzing your photos. There is a little known phenomena of luminous balls of light being seen at locations that may fall into the category of orbs, these are different than common orbs and are still not well understood by researchers and should not be confused with orbs found in photos. These could be naturally occurring ball lightning or plasma discharge and can be seen with the naked eye.

4: In the United States, there are no schools offering parapsychology courses. You MAY be able to find Internet classes from abroad, but please check credentials of the school before paying any money.

5: There is some evidence to suggest that adolescent females can cause poltergeist activity as well as people with untreated epilepsy. Also it is not uncommon for non-human entities to mimic this type of phenomenon. Please keep this in mind when dealing with this type of activity.

6: Some people believe that negative thoughts can create negative entities and that positive creates positive entities. PLPI finds this to be a bit egotistical in that humans are not God and therefore cannot create entities with conscious thought. Negative thoughts can feed negative entities thereby making them stronger and positive thought can weaken them, however putting ourselves in the role of "creator" seems wrong.

Bibliography/Resources

Alcatraz
bop.gov/about/history/alcatraz.jsp
www.geography.about.com/od/
unitedstatesofamerica/a/Alcatraz-Prison-Facts.htm
www.history.com/topics/alcatraz
www.nps.gov/alca/historyculture/index.htm
www.legendsofamerica.com/ca-alcatraz.html

Banning Residence Museum
www.en.wikipedia.org/wiki/Banning_House
www.socalhistory.org/biographies/phineas-banning.
html
www.bigorangelandmarks.blogspot.com/2007/05/
no-25-general-phineas-banning-residence.html

The Banta Inn
www.sanjoaquinmagazine.com/sanjoaquin/2010/10/
banta.html
www.mindreader.com/
pdfs/A%20GHOST%20AMONG%20THE%20SPIRITS.
pdf

Bodie Ghost Town
www.ghosttowns.com/states/ca/bodie.html
www.csicop.org/si/show/curse_of_bodie_legacy_
of_ghost-town_ghosts/
www.bodiehistory.com/
www.haunted-places-to-go.com/ghost-towns-1.html

Calico Ghost Town
www.ghosttowns.com/states/ca/calico.html
www.mouseplanet.com/beyond/bd010627.htm
www.legendsofamerica.com/ca-calico2.html
www.squidoo.com/the-ghosts-of-haunted-calico-
ghost-town

Camarillo State Hospital
www.users.resist.ca/~kirstena/pagecamarillo.html
www.weirdus.com/states/california/ghosts/
camarillo_state_hospital/
http://209.129.118.23/history/documents/history.
html

Casa de Estudillo
www.parks.ca.gov/?page_id=25398
www.hauntedhouses.com/states/ca/casa_de_
estudillo.html
www.san-diego-travels.com/casa-de-estudillo.html
www.sdjewishworld.wordpress.com/2010/04/30/
san-diegos-historic-places-casa-de-estudillo/

Drum Barracks
www.en.wikipedia.org/wiki/Drum_Barracks
www.californiahistorian.com/articles/drum-barracks.
html
www.militarymuseum.org/DrumBks.html
www.legendsofamerica.com/ca-drumbarracks.html

Fort MacArthur Museum
www.ftmac.org/Fmhist.html
www.militarymuseum.org/FtMacArthur.html
www.fortwiki.com/Fort_MacArthur

Gay Nineties Pizza Company
www.shoppleasanton.com/gayninetiespizza/?listing.
action=about

La Purisima State Historic Park
www.lapurisimamission.org/history-overview/
www.parks.ca.gov/?page_id=24893
www.athanasius.com/camission/purissima.htm
www.livescifi.tv/2011/08/haunted-la-purisima-
mission-history-ghosts-and-ghost-hunt-video-
archive/

Moss Beach Distillery
Morrall, June. *Moss Beach*. Charleston, South Carolina:
Arcadia Publishing, 2010.
www.mossbeachdistillery.com/our_story.html
www.hauntedbay.com/features/MBDistillery.shtml

Pleasanton Pioneer Cemetery
www.museumsrv.org/documents/TVdirectory1012011.
pdf
www.l-ags.org/cem_pd/pgintro.html
www.cityofpleasantonca.gov/pdf/pcsr-5a-cemetery.
pdf

Queen Mary
Harding, Steve. *Gray Ghost: The R.M.S. Queen Mary at
War*. Missoula, Montana: Pictorial Histories Publishing,
Co., 1982.
Steele, James. *Queen Mary*. London, England:
Phadidon Press, 2001.
www.queenmarystory.com/

Rancho Camulos
www.ranchocamulos.org/rancho_camulos_history.
html
www.nps.gov/history/nr/travel/american_latino_
heritage/Rancho_Camulos.html
www.scvhistory.com/scvhistory/camulos-nrhp3.htm
www.weirdca.com/location.php?location=76

San Francisco Maritime Museum
www.sf-waterfront.com/balclutha-sailing-ship%E2%80%94the-bay-areas-last-square-rigged-ship/
www.nps.gov/safr/historyculture/eureka-history.html
www.nps.gov/safr/historyculture/hercules-history.html

Shadow Ranch
www.laokay.com/halac/miscellaneousadobes.html
www.laparks.org/dos/historic/shadow.html
www.dailynews.com/20101030/those-who-seek-the-paranormal-are-convinced-la-is-a-real-live-ghost-town

Silver City Ghost Town
www.ghosttowns.com/states/ca/silvercity.html
www.lakeisabella.net/silvercity/
www.sierranevadageotourism.org/content/silver-city-ghost-town/sieDB34E22B7EE1111DA

Star of India
www.sdmaritime.org/star-of-india/
www.spiffingsailor.tumblr.com/post/3614287209
www.deadofnighttales.com/2012/06/haunted-ships-star-of-india-part-iii.html

The Anaheim White House
www.anaheimwhitehouse.com/#!about/c18zm
www.pdfhost.focus.nps.gov/docs/NRHP/Text/82000977.pdf
www.books.google.com/books?id=GsMwzukGmKMC&pg=PA157&lpg=PA157&dq=%2BThe+Anaheim+White+House%2BDr.+John+Truxaw&source=bl&ots=1FibirIhK8&sig=IKzBl2k6_8B9JFNI0TEILVwTRsO&hl=en&sa=X&ei=BTpDUv3WIMm8iwKT0oCYDg&ved=0CDUQ6AEwAQ#v=onepage&q=%2BThe%20Anaheim%20White%20House%2BDr.%20John%20Truxaw&f=false

USS Hornet
www.cva-12.com
www.uss-hornet.org
www.usshornetmuseum.org
www.its.caltech.edu/~drmiles/ghost_stories.html

Vallecito Stage Stop
www.legendsofamerica.com/ca-vallecito.html
www.desertusa.com/mag98/oct/stories/stagecoach.html
www.abdnha.org/TSP-vallicito-destination-along-the-emigrant-route.html
www.sandiegofamily.com/travel/one-day-trips/82-the-journey-of-death-valley

Warner Grand Theater
www.grandvision.org/warner-grand/history.asp
www.en.wikipedia.org/wiki/Warner_Grand_Theatre
www.articles.latimes.com/1996-09-18/local/me-44977_1_san-pedro

Whaley House
www.whaleyhouse.org/historyrestoration.html
www.piratebooty.net/whaleyhouse/whaleyhistory.html
www.sohosandiego.org/main/historywh.html
www.sandiegohistory.org/journal/60april/whaley.html

Planet Paranormal Websites
www.planetparanormal.com
www.parainvestigations.com
www.queenmaryshadows.com